♥♣♦♠ THE ♠♦♣♥

BEST HAND I EVER PLAYED

52 WINNING POKER LESSONS
FROM THE WORLD'S GREATEST PLAYERS

♥♣♦♠ THE ♠♦♣♥

BEST HAND I EVER PLAYED

52 WINNING POKER LESSONS
FROM THE WORLD'S GREATEST PLAYERS

STEVE ROSENBLOOM

ESPN
BOOKS

ISBN 1-933060-03-4

ESPN books are available for special promotions and premiums.
For details contact Michael Rentas, Assistant Director
Inventory Operations, Hyperion
77 West 66th Street, 11th floor
New York, New York 10023
or call 212-456-0133.

BOOK DESIGN: Eric Baker Design Associates / Eric Baker with Christopher Lee

FIRST EDITION
10 9 8 7 6 5 4 3 2 1

To Ellen, my mother, the first gambler I ever knew, and still one of the best.

To Jerry, my late father, who used to cry at stoplights, so he certainly would be flooding the room over this.

To Brandon, who does not appear to need this book to turn a profit at Hold'em.

To Allison, who said, "Dad, I don't play poker, so I don't think I'll read your book," and then paused, arched an eyebrow, and asked with a smile, "but who are you going to dedicate the book to?"

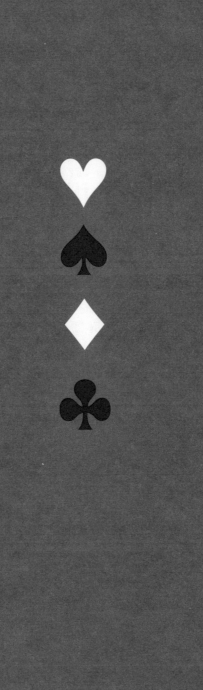

♠◆ CONTENTS ♥♣

Introduction 11
Note to Readers 13

♥♣◆♠ THE ♠◆♣♥
BEST HAND I EVER PLAYED

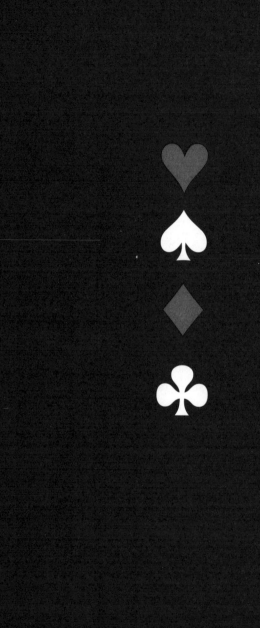

♠♦ INTRODUCTION ♥♣

If you want to learn how to play poker the way the big-time players do—or even if you just want to run over your pals in a weekly home game—you have to learn from the best in the world. Learn the way they think, learn the way they play hands, learn the way they fold them, and learn the way they break down specific opponents and situations.

That was the idea when I began writing a weekly poker column for the *Chicago Tribune*, and that's the idea behind this book. On the following pages, fifty-two of the world's greatest players will set up the best hand in their storied careers, explain how they made their decisions, and analyze the results. There is a lesson in every one of them—what I have called "The Rake." In some cases, you will find an approach you might never have considered. In others, you will learn the stories behind the stories you saw on television. In still others, you will learn how the best players in the world balance mathematical odds, physical tells, and pure instinct.

You will no doubt be surprised by many of the choices some made, especially the ones who said the best hand they ever played involved pots they didn't actually win. In those cases, they might have made every right move to set up an opponent, only to have the wrong card fall. Or they might have lost a pot because they folded before they risked losing their tournament lives. That kind of thinking offers you the chance to improve your game, because in poker, it's often worth losing a little now to win a lot later.

You'll notice I begin each chapter with a short biography of each player. Two reasons for that: First, when you realize how these people have come from such different backgrounds, I hope it will humanize them more than the often cartoonish personas you see on television—and perhaps you will even find it less intimidating to think of sitting across the table from them. Second, I like these people. A lot. And I wanted you to have the chance to like them as well. In this exploding era of poker-palooza, they are remarkably generous with their time and with their willingness to offer insight into the game they love—even if it might be viewed as giving away trade secrets.

I hope you learn as much from the experts in this book as I have over the years. And who knows, maybe you'll become a chapter in the next one.

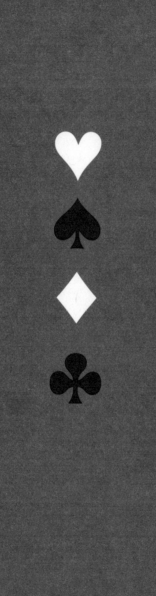

♠♦ NOTE TO READERS ♥♣

In each chapter of *The Best Hand I Ever Played*, you will notice that some words are highlighted in red. These words will be defined on the page, but can also be found in the glossary in the back. Words that are highlighted in **gray** have been previously defined on the page, but can also be found in the glossary in the back. And any player's name in **bold-faced type** signifies that the player's best hand also appears in the book.

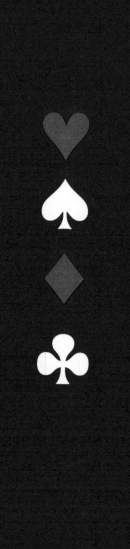

♥♦♦♠ THE ♠♦♦♥
BEST HAND I EVER PLAYED

♠♦ JOSH ARIEH ♥♣

JOSH ARIEH LIKES TO TALK TRASH—THAT'S JUST PART OF HIS GAME.
Like the time in the 2004 World Series of Poker main event he
went all in to beat Harry Demetriou, and then derided Demetriou
for the way he played the hand.

"I come from the pool room, man," the thirty-year-old
Arieh says in a plaintive, raspy voice, "and all my life, when people beat me bad, they talked shit. It's part of competition. I love
competition. I love winning and I love sticking the needle in and
making it worse. Because losing hurts. Losing really hurts, you
know? The old saying of, 'it's not whether you win or lose, but how you
play the game'—no, it's winning. That's why they have championships. That's why they
have playoffs. Losing really, really hurts."

The Georgia-based Arieh, who started atlantapokerschool.com, has certainly had his
share of each. "I was young when I first came out," he says. "I played at a final table [in
1999] with **Howard Lederer**, John Juanda, Humberto Brenes, Tom Franklin, all sea-
soned pros, and I won. I'm gonna talk shit. If people at home were trying to figure who'd
win, I wasn't on anybody's list, and I rose above it. It's the pinnacle of what you do.
You're at home playing house games, and then you're at the final table of the World
Series. I was there and I beat them, and I was happy."

But when Arieh finished third at the 2004 WSOP to **Greg Raymer** (who said Arieh
was the player he feared the most), he took the loss hard. "I won $2.5 million and I was
out on the street in front of the Horseshoe crying my eyes out. It wasn't first. I didn't
win. It's a lot of money, yeah, but I still got knocked out. I'm more of a competitor than
I am a poker player."

Despite the tearful ending, Arieh says the best hand he ever played came during that
2004 World Series of Poker main event: "My table image was amazing. I didn't have to
play big pots. Nobody was getting in my way.

"My chip count was around $2 million. The average stack was around $1 million. With
two tables left, John Murphy, a kid who was playing great, raised. He made an average
raise. I had about the same amount of chips, and I called behind him with the K-4 of
hearts.

"Everybody else folded. The flop came Q-6-2, the 6 and 2 were hearts. He bet small,
real fast. Throughout the tournament, I hadn't been making many decisions on the
flop. I was playing position and forcing my opponent to act in front of me on the turn.
That way I get more information on the hand.

"He made a small bet that didn't tell me much on the flop. I called quickly. I mean, I have a flush draw. I'm not necessarily trying to make my flush. I'm trying to get more information from him to where maybe I can represent something and maybe I can steal from him."

The turn came a jack of clubs. Murphy bet $300,000, about three-quarters the size of the pot. "Now I figured that he had a hand, but if I made mine, I figured I get paid off. I figured that my implied pot odds were great because if he has a hand and I make my flush, I'd win all his chips."

The river came a queen of hearts, giving Arieh a flush. "I made what I was trying to make, and he bet all in. He counted it and it was almost exactly what I had. It would've left me crippled for the tournament. And my goal in the World Series wasn't to try to win a big pot like that. I just wanted to win small pots, chop away, chop away, and now I'm faced with this big decision.

"There was a chance I had the best hand. I thought it was about 80 percent that I had the best hand and 20 percent that I had the worst hand. The 20 percent that I could be wrong totally outweighed the 80 percent. If I'm wrong this one time, I'm done."

Murphy was holding a full house, 2's full of queens, and Arieh, despite having made the flush he wanted, still folded—perhaps the best laydown in the main event.

"For that one week, I felt that I was thinking so clearly. I had one goal in mind and I wasn't going to let the chance that I was wrong get in my way."

THE RAKE

The two lessons here are fairly basic, but inextricably linked: Know how to read the board and your opponent's betting pattern because these are the biggest pieces of information you will have at any table.

In this hand, the board read Q-6-2-J-Q, with three hearts. Murphy's betting pattern went like this: standard pre-flop raise, small bet on the flop, big bet on the turn, all in on the river.

Murphy's big bet on the turn meant one of two things: He actually had a hand or he was bluffing. You could characterize Murphy's play the same way on the river, but there was a big difference: The board paired. In this case, queens.

So if you're Josh Arieh, you have to go back to Murphy's opening move and ask this: Do you think he is the type of player who would make that pre-flop raise with J-Q? If so, then he has queens full of jacks.

But you can't limit your thinking to just that, especially when you're talking about the final two tables of the World Series of Poker main event. Nobody who gets there is simply lucky—everyone has game. Which means you then have to analyze your opponent by

World Series of Poker: The most famous poker tournament in the world. It began in 1970 when Benny Binion drew his Texas poker pals together at his Las Vegas casino, Binion's Horseshoe, for several days of several poker events. The champion was determined by a vote of the players. Poker legend Johnny Moss was the first champion. After that, the champion became the player holding all the chips in the final event, which cost $10,000 to enter. The buy-in for the main event remains $10,000, but there are more than thirty events at different buy-in levels for which the winner gets a gold bracelet. Abbreviated to WSOP. **All in:** To move all of your chips into the pot, putting your tournament life at stake. **Table image:** How you are perceived in a game based on your personality and your betting habits. For instance, a loose-aggressive table image comes from playing or raising almost as many hands as a maniac, while a weak-tight player has a table image of playing only premium hands and not playing them as aggressively. **Flop:** The first three common cards in Hold'em and Omaha, which are revealed at once. **Turn:** The fourth of five common cards turned face up in Hold'em and Omaha. Also known as fourth street. **Flush draw:** Four cards to complete a flush.

Implied pot odds: Not just the amount of money in the pot, but the additional amount you can reasonably expect to be bet into the pot by the end, based on the way players have represented their hands so far. Pot odds are the percentage of your chances of hitting an unseen card that can make your hand vs. the cost of your bet compared to amount of money in the pot. Implied pots odds are the percentage of your chances of hitting an unseen card compared to the cost of your bet vs. the amount of money that will be in the pot by the end. **River:** The last card dealt in a poker hand. In Hold'em and Omaha, it also known as fifth street. **Board:** The common cards turned face up. **Pre-flop:** The first round of betting; before the first three community cards are exposed. **Pocket pair:** Matching cards in the hole. **Wired pair:** Same as a pocket pair.

asking this: Is Murphy the kind of player who would make that opening move and follow through to an all in with a pocket pair of any board card? Because any wired pair of jacks, 6's or, yes, deuces, gives Murphy a full house.

If you don't think so, then you call his bluff. But if his betting pattern fits the way he has previously played pocket pairs—and if it fits that pattern strongly enough to give you doubts about risking your tournament life—then you give up a very good hand with the discipline and instincts that every top player has.

Arieh played position perfectly. He was able to act last with every piece of information available. So, when he drew out to the flush he was looking for, he had gained enough information to think—correctly, as it turned out—that Murphy had the best hand.

♠♦ JOE AWADA ♥♣

JOE AWADA'S ALL-AMERICAN SUCCESS STORY BEGINS IN BEIRUT, LEBANON.
"I came here when I was thirteen," he says. "My mom brought me and my sister, left me in Toledo, Ohio, with my uncle, and went back with my sister. We were trying to get the rest of the family over."

Young Joe was told to work hard so they could send money back home to bring over his brothers and sisters. His uncle, meanwhile, was on the concession staff of the Ringling Bros. and Barnum and Bailey circus, so Awada joined the circus and started selling balloons, cotton candy, and ice cream.

"I decided I could do better than concessions," he explains, and so he became a juggler. "I was practicing every day for two years while I was selling. I became good enough to be in the American Continental Circus out of California.

"I got better and better and made it to Vegas, performed in a lot shows at the Flamingo, Sahara, Circus Circus. Then I had a car accident and couldn't juggle any-more, so I got into gaming." The one-time card dealer, slots supervisor and pit boss likes to joke that he's been in the industry so long that he goes back to a time when poker was dying.

Now married and the father of six, the forty-seven-year-old Awada is the CEO and president of his own gaming company, which creates table and video games for casinos, including Three Way Action, which combines War, Blackjack and Seven Card Stud. And, oh yes, in his spare time he's a professional poker player. Awada logged a lot of television time during the 2004 World Series of Poker, beating colorful Danish star **Marcel Luske** for the $5,000 buy-in Seven Card Stud bracelet after finishing second to **Scott Fischman** in the $1,500 buy-in No Limit Hold'em event.

Interestingly, the erstwhile dealer Awada says the best hand he ever played came against another former dealer, Fischman, when they were heads-up at the final table of the No Limit Hold'em event.

"The greatest hand I ever played turned out to be not a happy ending," he says. "I had a small chip lead, and I felt I had a very good read on Scott. The whole night I felt I was reading everyone well—I was correct on every occasion. There were a couple of times where I laid down big hands."

Awada had pocket 5's. Fischman held A-K and raised pre-flop. Awada called. The flop came 9-4-7. Fischman moved all in.

"The way he said 'Aall in,' I could see he had no confidence in that—the tone of his voice, the way he did it, his facial reaction," Awada says. "It's hard to explain, but I can tell even more from a side facial than I can from face up. Some guys wear the glasses and it's really hard. What helps me is when I look at the side facial. I can see something. I can't explain it, but I really can. So I was comfortable with the fact that I thought he had either A-Q, A-J, or A-K.

"That was a big call for me to make. But after seeing the flop, I have a bigger advantage than a coin flip. There were only two cards left. That puts you at 3-1 or 4-1. I thought a little bit and I was comfortable with it. I go with what I read and I called him."

The turn came a 9 for a board of 9-7-4-9. "He needed a 7. A 9, he would lose. A 4, he would lose. He's got six cards between the ace and the king, then he's got three more cards with the 7 (because he could make two pair with a better kicker).

"The river came a 7, and he won with the ace-high kicker. I read it right. I made the right play. Regardless of whether you win or lose, the way I see it, it doesn't matter past that point. I made the right decision.

"I came back to win a bracelet in the Seven Card Stud world championship, but by taking that bad beat it brought me so much more popularity, not only for me personally, but also my business. That is advertising I can never buy."

THE RAKE

One of the tough facts of poker is that you will get beat badly sometimes. Maybe lots of times, maybe at the worst possible time, almost like it's a commandment. But understand that bad beats are a part of the game, and how you handle them will make you a better player. Awada's grace under monstrously difficult circumstances—one card away from a World Series bracelet—bought him wonderful respect that has, he says, spilled over into his business ventures. He also composed himself well enough to play championship poker in winning the Seven Card Stud bracelet event.

Seven Card Stud: Each player receives his first two cards down, the next four cards up, and the last card down. There is a round of betting after each up card and the last down card. Players use the seven cards to make the best five-card hand. **Heads-up:** Playing one-on-one; usually referring to the last two players in a tournament. **Bad beat:** To lose a hand when you are the favorite. It's particularly bad when it happens on the river. **Overpair:** Matching hole cards that are higher than the best card on the board.

"I love the guy," Fischman says. "He's awesome. That was the first day I met him, but now we're good friends. No hard feelings, and he went on to get his own bracelet the next week."

Perhaps the only thing Awada did better than handle himself with class was play the hand to put himself in position to win. Awada's pair of 5's was a 55-45 pre-flop favorite over Fischman's A-K. After the flop missed both players, Awada was a 3-1 favorite. When Fischman went all in, Awada had good odds to win the hand and the tournament. What's more, because poker is about people, Awada took a read on Fischman and became convinced that Fischman's body language told him he wasn't holding an overpair.

Then, when the turn came a 9, Awada was a dominating 4-1 favorite. The deck just came badly for him when a 7 fell, creating a board of two pair higher than Awada's 5's and having it come down to the kicker—Fischman's ace. If you can make the right read and the right call the way Awada did, the odds say you will be playing championship-caliber poker.

♠♦ LYLE BERMAN ♥♣

YOU MIGHT NOT KNOW LYLE BERMAN, BECAUSE YOU DON'T SEE HIM ON TELEVISION MUCH. But you certainly see what he puts on TV: the World Poker Tour.

"Ever since I started playing in 1983, I felt that poker could be a good TV sport if you showed the hole cards," the Minnesota-born Berman says. "I looked into it a little bit, but the timing wasn't right. Then, of course, Steve Lipscomb brought me a business plan in 2002 to create the World Poker Tour. I believed in it. I took it to my board of directors [at Lakes Entertainment]. They liked it, and the rest is kind of history."

The bespectacled, balding Berman, who graduated in 1964 from the University of Minnesota with a degree in business administration, has shown he knows how to make money as the house. He also has shown he knows how to do it at the tables.

Berman owns three World Series of Poker bracelets—one for Limit Omaha, one for No Limit Hold'em, one for Deuce-to-Seven Draw—and plays in some of the biggest cash games around. In 2002, he was inducted into the Poker Hall of Fame at Binion's Horseshoe, and the casino honored him by slapping his face on a $5 chip.

"As a kid, I played a whole lot of poker," Berman says. "I actually was thrown out of Wharton in my junior year for running a poker game with my two roommates in our apartment.

World Poker Tour: An international circuit of poker events that is broadcast on the Travel Channel. It was created in 2002 and revolutionized televised poker through the use of tiny cameras that reveal each player's hole cards. **House:** Another name for the casino; the host of the game. **Limit Omaha:** Limit poker is a game that has preset betting amounts. For example, a $10-$20 game means bets or raises are limited to $10 on the first two rounds, then increase to $20 on the next two rounds. Omaha is a game where you are dealt four hole cards with five cards to be turned face up as in Hold'em—three cards on the flop and one each on the turn and the river—but you must use exactly two cards from your hand and exactly three cards from the board to make your five-card poker hand.

"I started working and quit playing. Then in 1983, I read **Doyle Brunson**'s book *Super/System*. I came out [to Las Vegas] and started playing in some tournaments and just kept playing." More than twenty years after reading Brunson's seminal book, Berman—whose son Bradley is also a big-time poker player—was asked to write a chapter for the sequel *Super/System 2* on Pot Limit Omaha High.

A character you would expect to find in the colorful world of poker, Berman says the best hand he ever played came in a No Limit Hold'em cash game at the Frontier Hotel in the late 1980s.

"I had the Q-J of spades. I bet, a guy raised, and I called. Turned out he had two aces," Berman says. "The flop came A-10-3 of spades. We each had about $50,000. I bet about $10,000 on the flop, and he raised like $25,000. I moved all in. He called. We had about $100,000 in the pot. Obviously, I had a spade flush and he had three aces."

The turn came the 10 of diamonds, pairing the board and giving Berman's opponent a full house, aces full of 10's.

"The river came the king of spades, and I had a royal flush. That's pretty hard to even write that story, let alone believe it really happened. When the king came, I didn't even realize it had given me a royal flush. If somebody wrote that one in Hollywood, they'd say, 'You can't believe that.' "

THE RAKE

Sometimes the cards just come right for you and leave the other guy with as bad a beat as you can imagine. Fine. You're owed that much, right?

The instructive thing is how Berman played after the flop, one of the most critical abilities you can develop in poker. The influence of the television editing process makes it seem as if the undeniable drama of someone going all in pre-flop happens every other hand. The truth is, it doesn't. Mostly, that's a rookie mistake, largely because betting after the flop is so intricate and requires much more attention to putting an opponent on a hand and evaluating the strength of your own.

Berman flopped a flush—the third-nut flush with a queen-high—which is a powerful hand. He wasn't trying to get all his money into the pot—he could have done that by going all in immediately—as much as he was trying to get all his opponent's money into it. So he bet $10,000 as a way of inducing his opponent to play back at him if he had an ace, a way of determining the type of hand he was up against. When his opponent came over the top with a $25,000 raise, Berman was convinced that his opponent had a hand he would bet his entire stack on, so he moved in and got the call he was looking for.

Credit Berman's opponent for having the ability to play after the flop, as well. He could have gone all in on Berman's $10,000 bet, figuring his aces made the best hand. But he, too, wanted to make sure all the money got into the pot, so he raised enough to make Berman think there was a big hand out there, but not enough to run him out completely. How in the world would Berman's opponent have figured he would drown on the river amid a royal flush?

The point is, both players demonstrated a highly successful tight-aggressive approach: When you play a hand that you think is the best, play it to get all the money in the middle.

Deuce-to-Seven Draw: A type of lowball where the best hand—in this case, 7-5-4-3-2—would be the worst in most other games. Games with a draw allow you to throw away cards from your hand and be dealt the same number of new cards from the deck. **Cash game:** The most conventional form of poker, whether it is in a casino or your basement. You buy chips and play. If you go broke, you can buy more chips. In a tournament, when you go broke, you leave the table. Cash games also are referred to as side games. **Royal flush:** The highest possible hand in poker, consisting of the A-K-Q-J-10 of the same suit. **Putting an opponent on a hand:** The ability to determine which cards another player is holding based on his betting pattern, the position at the table from which he is making those bets, and his history of betting in other situations. You are trying to figure out how strong or weak a hand you're up against. **Third-nut flush:** The nuts are the best possible hand based on what the board is showing. If there are three spades exposed, but none is the ace, then holding the ace along with another card of the same suit gives you the nut flush. If the ace of spades is exposed, then the king is the nut card because it is the highest possible spade not on the board that would make the flush. If you hold the queen and another suited card in that case, you have the third-nut flush card. **Play back:** To reraise an opponent. Sometimes it is done to reinforce strength, sometimes it is done to make an opponent doubt the strength of his hand.. **Come over the top:** To re-raise a huge amount, usually all in. **Drown on the river:** To lose on the last common card turned face up. Where bad beat stories are made.

♠♦ DOYLE BRUNSON ♥♣

THE MAN WITH THE TRADEMARK COWBOY HAT AT THE POKER TABLE ALMOS BECAME the man in the shorts on an NBA court. Indeed, poker legend Doyle Brunson was such a terrific athlete that he was scouted by the Lakers back when they were still in Minneapolis. And despite having a distinctive first name that could have predated the championship likes of Shaq, Kobe, Magic and Kareem, Doyle never went pro because of a knee injury.

Instead, the owner of a sharp math mind turned to selling business machines, but found there was more money to be made putting those math skills to work at poker. So, he lit out of his small Texas hometown of Longworth and became a road gambler, driving from town to town with other legendary poker figures **Thomas "Amarillo Slim" Preston** and Brian "Sailor" Roberts, looking for big poker games, then driving some more when they had cleaned out the town.

Honing his craft and gaining a reputation as big as the Stetson he often wears, "Texas Dolly" even has a hand named after him: 10-2. That's a "Doyle Brunson," because that was the final hand he played at the final table in winning back-to-back World Series of Poker championships in 1976 and 1977.

Following his second WSOP title, Brunson, who owns a record-tying nine World Series of Poker bracelets, published his groundbreaking book *Super/System* on power poker, still considered the bible for card players. The seventy-two-year-old Brunson, who plays in the biggest cash games around, has also entered the modern age with an Internet poker site called—what else?—Doylesroom.com.

Brunson says the best hand he ever played came nearly fifty years ago, long before he won those back-to-back World Series of Poker championships. Heck, it came even before there *was* a World Series of Poker. But that hand, he believes, was the one that helped him get those bracelets and the millions he has won.

It came against Johnny Moss, a Hall of Fame player who was awarded the championship trophy at the first World Series of Poker in a vote of the players in 1970 (the World Series did not begin its current freeze-out tournament form until the next year). "I was twenty-four or twenty-five years old at that point and still kind of new," Brunson says. "Johnny Moss was the best. He and I were really fierce competitors from the beginning because I think he recognized that I was going to be the next top player, so he tried especially hard against me.

"Johnny had a lot more money than I had, so Johnny could money-whip me. He could make situations where it was hard for me to call because he had so much money and I didn't have that much.

"This was a cash game in Texas. There weren't any tournaments in those days. The guy in the first seat made a small bet about the size of the pot. Johnny Moss called it. I had a J-10."

The flop came K-7-8. Brunson thought Moss was drawing at a straight. The turn came a 2, and everybody checked. The river came a 3.

"The first guy checked and Moss made some kind of real big bet, and I thought to myself he was drawing at a straight and he missed it and he thinks he's going to win this pot. I called with just the jack-high. The other guy paired kings and threw that away. Johnny was drawing at a small straight.

"That was my greatest hand because I think that kind of defined the moment that I became what I knew was a real top player."

THE RAKE

Poker is about heart: having the heart to go with your gut in calling down a master player with just a jack-high. "You have to have that competitive spirit," Brunson says. "I don't know what it is. I can't define it. It's an innate ability in you that surfaces in times of stress and hard situations, and that's the difference. It's nothing you can explain."

If Moss had been holding just a deuce, then the deuce on the turn would have made him nearly a 4-1 favorite. For that matter, if Moss had been holding just a queen, Brunson loses. And when the board failed to pair, Moss' bet could've been interpreted as the last chance to get paid off on a pair of kings. In all, almost half the cards in the deck had Brunson beat.

When the man with the bigger stack made a major bet into a hand without so much as a pair, the money play, it seems, would have been to muck. But Brunson had a read on Moss. It was a combination of Moss' betting pattern—many players with busted flushes and straights tend to make a big play for a pot that gets checked down to the end—and Moss' history of money-whipping. Brunson had the heart to stick with his read on Moss and not bow to the odds against him.

First seat: Also known as first position, it is the first player to act in a given round of betting. **Bet into:** To bet ahead of the player who has represented the strongest hand. **Muck:** To fold a hand; "the muck" refers to the pile of cards that are folded or unused.

This is the first hard lesson in poker: balancing the contradictory dogma of the read versus the science of the math—what your gut tells you about whether you have the best hand versus what the pot odds and betting patterns tell you about it.

Poker is, of course, about people, starting with yourself. You must have the heart to play your cards against a big raise or a scary board if you believe you have the best of it. If you shrink when facing adversity—and every player faces it, even Doyle Brunson—you don't stand a chance.

♠♦ "MIAMI" JOHN CERNUTO ♥♣

WITH HIS STOCKY BODY AND EXPRESSIVE FACE, "MIAMI" JOHN CERNUTO could be a dead ringer for Lou Costello. Or maybe Buddy Hackett. And like those two great comedians, Cernuto can be just as charismatic and funny whether he's winning or losing. The Jersey-born Cernuto graduated from Florida State University with a finance degree, then after a stint in the Army and some time as a repo man, he took a job with the Federal Aviation Administration.

"I did that until August 3, 1981," Cernuto says with precision, remembering the exact day that the air traffic controllers went on strike—two days later, they were fired by President Reagan. And so, after years of looking after the lives of passengers, he had to get on with his own.

Cernuto says he took his government retirement check in hand and some money from the bank, and headed to Las Vegas. "I thought I was going to make it as a professional poker player, but I really didn't know squat about being one," he says. "I'd never played Hold'em before, except for High-Low Split Hold'em, so I really didn't have a good background in that.

"I learned at the school of hard knocks. Experience was probably my best teacher. After about two and a half years, I went broke. The money ran out. I took a job dealing at the Stardust, but I got disgusted with that. Then I went back to Daytona Beach where my mother lived and got a job as a police dispatcher for nine months. Got disgusted with that. Then I borrowed $600 from my parents, drove back to Las Vegas, and got a job dealing at the Las Vegas Hilton."

About a year later, Cernuto won his first big poker tournament, the Seven Card Stud event in Amarillo Slim's Super Bowl of Poker, collecting $50,000. "That was the first time I ever used the name 'Miami John,'" Cernuto says. "I worked in Miami for a long time, so I used that name because there were several people who used cities in their name, and I said, 'Let me try something,' because I'd never won a major tournament. I never lost a pot the whole day—I had to keep the name."

It certainly paid off: Since adopting the moniker, Cernuto has won three World Series of Poker bracelets in such varied games as Hold'em, Omaha and Stud High-Low. But Cernuto says the best hand he ever played came in a $300-$600 Omaha 8-or-Better cash game at the Bellagio.

"I've been getting killed in this game all day. I played a hand with A-2-3-8. The flop came down J-7-8, two diamonds. I'm trying for the low. The next card was a big diamond. I still had the low hand and the phony flush." (The phony flush is where you hold the ace of the suit that's on the board, but you don't have another card in that suit in your hand. In Omaha, you have to use two cards from your hand and three from the board, but you bet the phony flush as if you have two cards of that suit in your hand.)

Cernuto bet. The first player to his left called. The next guy called. The next player also called. The last player raised. "I don't have my low. I don't have a flush," Cernuto says. "There's already now about $4,000 in the pot. I decided I was going to represent the nut flush. I re-raised $600. Three guys called, one folded."

The river came a king. Cernuto bet. The first player to his left folded. The next player also folded. "There's one more guy left, and this guy had been my nemesis for years. I said, Oh, my god. I raised out all these hands that were better, and this SOB is probably going to win the pot with kings up. He thought and he thought and he thought, and he finally folded, and I won this huge pot with ace-high.

"I already knew one guy on my left had a straight. Another guy on my left said he had three jacks. The next guy says, 'I had three jacks beat; I had a small diamond flush.' So I got away from a straight, a set, and another flush, and my nemesis. He never told me what he had. My reputation of usually having good hands got me a pot.

"It was my greatest hand because it was my greatest bluff. It feels good—really good—when you get to bluff everybody out of a pot that big and you get away with it on four or five different people. They all had you beat, they all gave you this pot. I felt like showing the bluff, but I thought, well, I might have to use it next time. I told everybody I had the nuts."

THE RAKE

The play is called the Phony Ace, and it can get tricky in Omaha 8-or-Better. You start with having the ace of the suit that's on the board, but you don't have another card from that same suit in your hand. So the reason it is a Phony Ace is that in Omaha, you have to use two cards—and only two cards—from your hand along with three cards—and only three cards—from the board to make the best five-card poker hand.

For instance, if Cernuto had A-4 of diamonds in his hand and three diamonds come out, he has the nut flush. In this case, he had the ace of diamonds but no other card from that suit.

No matter. He bet like he had it. And he bet strong. The first key point is Cernuto's reputation as a world-class Omaha 8-or-Better player. His table image is further enhanced by his history of playing hands aggressively. But the most useful part of this hand is that once Cernuto decided to bluff, he played it the way he would have played the hand if he actually *had* the flush and bet consistent with his history in those situations. He re-raised on the turn, then followed by betting out on the river. Many players bluff at a pot once. But the best players—those with the heart to—fire twice. And they are probably getting good pot odds to do it.

High-Low Split: The highest hand splits the pot with the lowest hand. **Omaha-8-or-Better:** Played like straight Omaha—four hole cards, five board cards, you must use exactly two cards from your hand and exactly three cards from the board to make your five-card poker hand—but the pot is split between the best high hand and the best low hand. The low hand, however, must start with a card no higher than an 8 (i.e., 8-5-6-2-A. Straights and flushes are irrelevant when determining the low hand. You can use the same cards to make your low hand and your high hand, or different cards for each half of the pot. For instance, A-2-3-4-5 can be used as the best low hand and a straight for the high hand. If there is no low hand, the high hand wins the pot. **Kings up:** A hole card that matches the highest card on an unpaired board. If that card is a king, a player with only a king would have kings up. If it is an ace, a player with only an ace would have aces up, and so on. **Set:** Three of a kind. **Nuts:** The best possible hand.

♠ ♦ JOHNNY CHAN ♥ ♣

IN ORDER TO BECOME THE SUPERHERO KNOWN AS SUPERMAN CLARK KENT TOOK OFF his glasses and business suit. In order to become the poker superstar known as the Orient Express, Johnny Chan took off his apron.

Born in China, Chan moved to the United States with his family when he was nine—"the American dream," he says—and helped as his family opened a restaurant. But the real action started when the restaurant closed.

"We'd get enough players—the busboys, the waiters—that we all played all night, then we slept for a few hours and we opened the restaurant. Then we'd close and we'd play again," Chan says. "That was my schedule on the weekends."

In those days, after Chan won a lot of money in his adopted hometown of Houston, he would head to Las Vegas to see how he could do in casino table games, taking junkets when he was just sixteen.

"Just put up $2,500, and they'd give you airfare, room and board for three nights," he recalls. "I was underage, but at the time, they didn't care. They'd give you a little tag and it was like, 'Mr. C, how much you need?' 'Give me a marker for $500.' I was sixteen years old at the Landmark. I'd come out, put up my $2,500, go broke every time. Never win.

"For a gambler, you have to be a loser to become a winner. That was getting my experience, which was good. I don't regret it. I learned a lot. One trip I came out and went broke in two hours. I had nothing to do, so I went downtown, walked around and went into the Golden Nugget. I didn't know there was a poker room. I watched those guys play and I said, 'I could beat those guys.' Next thing you know, I took my gold necklace to a pawn shop and hocked it. They gave me $200. That was enough to buy in at the $10-$20 game at the Nugget. I ran that $200 to $30,000 in a week. I said, 'Wow, this is all right. I think I'm going to move out here.' That's how I started."

And he has not stopped. Chan has captured a record-tying nine World Series of Poker bracelets and became one of the few back-to-back winners of the WSOP world championship in 1987 and 1988. Many pros contend that Chan will be the last such back-to-back winner of the main event for a while, given the exploding fields in poker's greatest tournament.

Chan's greatness and inscrutable table image were further celebrated in the movie *Rounders*, a film he was urged to do by his daughter because she wanted to meet the star, Matt Damon.

For all of his tournament success, Chan says the best hand he ever played came during a cash game at the Bellagio: "We were playing $4,000-$8,000. I had pocket 8's. The other guy had pocket kings. I had position on him. He raised before the flop. I just called. The flop came 8-8-2.

"Any time you flop the stone nuts or such a big hand, the question is, how much money can I make on this? That's what I'm thinking. Trying to get the most value out of this hand.

"He bet. I called. He was so far behind. It's like you and I running a mile, and I'm already at the finish line and you're way back. I have to be like a turtle and just slow down.

"The turn came a king. Once he caught something, he started betting. He bet, I raised. He re-raised. I just called." The river came another 2 for a board of 8-8-2-K-2. Chan bet.

"He raised. I raised. He never stopped. And I never stopped, either. We put in about ten bets there. The total pot was probably about $300,000.

"When I play, I like to get position on my opponent, so this way they make a move first. If I knew my opponent has one move, one speed—they don't know the amounts to bet, they go all in—anytime I have the nuts on the flop or fourth street, I check because I know on fifth street they go all in, and I can go, 'I guess I call because I have the nuts.'"

Stone nuts: The absolutely the best possible hand. **Fourth Street:** See turn. **Fifth Street:** See river. **Quads over quads:** A four-of-a-kind beating another four-of-a-kind.

THE RAKE

It's a pretty basic betting philosophy: You have to let your opponents catch up because you can't make any money if you're the only one with a strong hand and you come out betting.

The danger for Chan on this hand was that when a king fell on the turn, he could have lost quads over quads if another king came on the river. So he raised just to see how strong his opponent was and how strong his opponent wanted to play it. Chan's call of his opponent's re-raise did several things. First, it confused him.

Remember, Chan called pre-flop and called again on the flop, indicating some strength. Then Chan raised on the turn, showing more strength when a king fell, but his opponent was holding two of the other kings, so what in the world could Chan be betting on?

Chan's call on the turn also created a bigger pot that would prompt an opponent holding big cards to bet on the river, especially an opponent holding top set. The 2 on the river double-paired the board, which gave Chan's opponent the best full house with his pocket kings, and so he got into a raising war while still having no idea what Chan held.

♠♦ T.J. CLOUTIER ♥♣

A HULKING MAN WITH A BROAD CHEST, A JUTTING JAW, AND A GROWLING VOICE, T.J. Cloutier smacks of intimidation. Even his block of graying hair looks tough, every bit the former college and professional tight end.

In fact, after playing in the 1959 Rose Bowl with the University of California, Berkeley, Cloutier served hard time on the tundra of the Canadian Football League, once taking an elbow in the mouth so violently that it drove his teeth through his lips. Of course, they sewed it up on the sideline. Of course, he went back into the game.

Upon leaving pro ball because of bad knees, Cloutier eventually landed in Texas, where he lives today, working the oil fields until he discovered he could make more money playing poker. And so he became one of the legendary road gamblers.

Since 1983, when he first anted up in the World Series of Poker, Cloutier has cashed more than forty times. He has won five bracelets and has earned more than $3 million in WSOP play.

A co-author of several authoritative books on poker, the sixty-five-year-old Cloutier cites as the best hand he ever played one that offers an interesting lesson: "It was against Al Krux, a cash game at the Bicycle Club about ten years ago. No Limit Hold'em. He hadn't won a pot all day. He had, like, $445 left or something and he moved all in. The guy two to his left was getting a massage. He lifted his head up and looked at it and decided not to call and threw it away. The massage girl saw the hand too.

"It got around to me on the button. I had two 10's and I said, hell, I'll call him because this is his last money and he might not have too much. So I call. Now, the dealer didn't see that I made the call and she dropped the deck on the muck. That means she had to reshuffle all the cards.

"The flop came K-10-4. I had two 10's. I flopped three 10's. He had two kings, so he had flopped three kings. The fourth card was a 10, so I had four 10's and I beat him in this pot.

"But that's not the kicker. The kicker is, you remember the guy who was looking at his hand and getting a massage? He had the other two 10's and had thrown them away. He told us he had thrown two 10's away, and the massage girl said, 'This guy threw away two 10's.' So, that meant the dealer had to make a mistake and drop the deck and reshuffle those 10's back in for Al to lose this hand to me. It's the worst beat in the history of poker.

"Needless to say, I never won another hand that night, but I beat him out of his last $445. Story of a lifetime."

THE RAKE

A couple of things about bad beats: They happen to everyone, and some people ought to recheck the play of the hand to see if they were even winning at some point, because a lot of players think they suffered a bad beat when they lost to a hand that was better to start with. Losing a big hand when you were behind from the start is not only not a bad beat, but it also might make people question why you played the hand to the river in the first place.

For instance, if you held A-K offsuit against a pair of deuces and consider it a bad beat when the lowly ducks beat your Big Slick, better reconsider, and here's why: The deuces were about a 53-47 percent pre-flop favorite heads-up, so you were behind to start with. And if the board came 7-10-3-J-5 without a flush draw, then you were never ahead in the hand and yet you kept throwing money at the pot, trying to buy hope or something when what you really needed was a lesson from this book.

However, if the flop came A-K-Q rainbow and the turn came a blank—making you a killer 95-5 percent favorite—and the river came a deuce, then you have a bad beat to talk about.

Some people say hearing bad beat stories is like listening to someone talk about his fantasy league team. But the key to bad beats is how you deal with them mentally and emotionally. Bad beats have sent players on tilt since poker began. Players who suffered bad beats have lost their composure and subsequently lost their bankroll. So, if you take a bad beat, first take a deep breath. And then move on. That pot is gone. And here's another thing: Some other player at the table could suffer a bad beat on the next hand, and you have to be mentally and emotionally ready to pounce on him if he goes on tilt.

No Limit Hold'em: In Hold'em, players are dealt two hole cards, followed by a maximum of five board cards (the first three exposed cards are the flop, the next card is the turn, the final card is the river). There are four rounds of betting: After each player receives hole cards, the flop, the turn and the river. In No Limit, the minimum bet is the size of the big blind. The maximum is all your chips, and you can bet all of them at any time. **Offsuit:** Cards of different suits. **Ducks:** Another name for the 2 cards or deuces. **Big Slick:** A-K in the hole. **Rainbow:** A flop of three different suits. **Blank:** A card that does not affect the strength of a hand. **On tilt:** To play out of control, usually the result of a bad beat or a bad decision that cost a player a lot of chips.

♠♦ HOYT CORKINS ♥♣

WEARING HIS TRADEMARK BLACK COWBOY HAT AND MIRRORED GLASSES in front of his unreadable, impassive visage, Hoyt Corkins has a classic poker face. And a classic poker game built on aggressive play.

A gentleman down to the river, Corkins played tournament poker from 1989 to 1992, winning a bracelet in Pot Limit Omaha in the 1992 World Series of Poker, but leaned toward playing cash games for the next decade or so.

"It takes intense concentration to play high-stakes poker," Corkins says. "If you're playing medium-limit games, you can play more cards from more positions and you can win doing that." But the money has grown so big on the World Poker Tour and the World Series of Poker that Corkins (who hails from south Alabama, where he "lives in a county that has three stoplights") came back to the tournament scene in 2003.

Corkins says the best hand he ever played came during the final table of the World Poker Finals against tournament star Phil Hellmuth. "I had A-J of clubs on the button. He had a K-9 of hearts. Phil raised it about $45,000 from the cutoff. I smooth-called."

The flop came A-K-10, with two clubs, and Hellmuth checked. Corkins bet $80,000, and Hellmuth called. The turn came a king, giving Hellmuth a set. He checked to Corkins, who deliberated before checking himself.

"The river card came an ace, a lucky card for me," Corkins says. "Fills me up, aces full of kings. He had kings full of aces. He checked to me and I bet $125,000 on the river and he pays it off.

"That would be my best hand because at that particular point in the tournament, everybody was jockeying for position. There were four people left. It gave me the upper hand, chip-wise. I think it gave me a 2-1 chip lead over Phil. If he wins that pot, it would be the reverse. He'd have a 2-1 chip lead on me, and position means a lot."

Remarkably, Hellmuth remained under control after the painful and expensive beat, complimenting Corkins on his hand and refraining from the typically loud and out-sized act that has earned him the nickname Poker Brat.

"Phil wants to win so bad," the charitable Corkins says, "and he really is a nice guy. He just wants to win so bad. I don't know, maybe he tries to win so hard sometimes."

THE RAKE

The critical part of this hand came during post-flop play, specifically, betting on the turn, or in Corkins' case, not betting on it, even with aces and the nut-flush draw. Corkins knew there was still one more street where he could take down the pot if his hand was as good as he thought it might be.

When Corkins checked, he avoided betting into Hellmuth's trap of slow-playing a set of kings. If Corkins had bet there, Hellmuth would have played back at him big and possibly forced Corkins to fold a hand with a big pot out there.

At the same time, Corkins knew that if he bet and Hellmuth had had a 10 instead of a king, Hellmuth might not have called with the three overcards on the board. And if Hellmuth had had an ace, Corkins figured he would have gotten paid on the river with his solid jack kicker, and he certainly would have taken the pot if a club fell to complete the flush.

The big constant in the way Corkins figured each possibility was that he held position on Hellmuth, perhaps the biggest advantage in the game. Position figured big in several ways.

For starters, Corkins hadn't put Hellmuth on a hand by the turn, so he could wait for Hellmuth, who was forced to act first, to make a move that might give him a better idea of Hellmuth's holdings. Corkins avoided having to make a bet that might run Hellmuth out of the pot or, worse, might run himself into Hellmuth's big holdings and face folding.

Second, Corkins' position also gave him the advantage of being able to get away from his hand if he wasn't helped on the river and faced a big bet from Hellmuth. In all, Corkins bet when he had the best hand on the flop, checked when he didn't have the best hand on the turn, and bet when he had the best hand on the river. That's as good as it gets.

Pot Limit: A game where the biggest bet cannot exceed the amount of money in the pot. Pot Limit games frequently reach No Limit-like proportions by the river. **Medium-limit:** Generally refers to games with $20-$40 and $30-$60 betting limits. **Cutoff:** The table position one to the right of the dealer button. **Smooth-call:** To match an opponent's bet. It is usually made by a player who would ordinarily consider raising. **Slow-playing:** To pass on opening the betting despite holding a powerful hand. It's usually done with aces or kings, or after flopping a set or a nut flush. The idea is to induce a player with lesser holdings to read you as weak in order to trap the player into betting. **Overcard:** A card in your hand that is higher than any card on the board, or a card on the board that is higher than the best card in your hand. **Kicker:** An unmatched card used to break ties.

♠♦ KASSEM "FREDDY" DEEB ♥♣

FOR A GUY WHO NEVER FINISHED COLLEGE, KASSEM DEEB SURE HAS been schooling opponents ever since. Born in Lebanon, Deeb came to the United States when he was nineteen, enrolling at Utah State University to study mechanical engineering.

"I didn't have many classes left to finish school, but the civil war broke out back home in Lebanon and I couldn't get any more money from home to go to school," he says. "Then I started gambling, and I never went back."

Deeb tried to get a job, but was unable to work in the United States because he held only a student visa. So he went into business for himself playing poker and never went back to school.

The diminutive, likable Deeb is a regular in the high-limit games at the Bellagio. He calls it "investing."

"I make all my money in cash games," Deeb, now forty-nine, says. "I've made a lot of final tables, but I don't play many tournaments. The last two years, I tried to play all the big tournaments—there's a lot of dead money."

Oh, and how did someone with the given name Kassem (pronounced kuh-SEEM) get the name "Freddy"? "One time a guy went to put my name on the list to play poker in Reno," Deeb explains. "He said, 'What's your name?' I said, 'Kassem—K-a-s-s-e-m.' So he starts to spell it, and after about nine times he couldn't get it right. Finally, my friend standing next to me says, 'His name is Freddy.' So he put down 'Freddy.' The next night I come in and he says, 'Freddy, you want to be on the list?' I said yeah. The next night I come in, and I end up living there. So every night, everybody starts calling me Freddy. A lot of people still don't know my real name."

What they do know is Deeb's wardrobe, specifically the red and white shirt he wore during the main event of the 2003 World Series of Poker in a hand he played against poker superstar and sometime fashion critic Phil Ivey. That shirt came courtesy of Deeb's mom, who brought several of them on a visit from Lebanon. "That day, I just happened to put that one on," Deeb says. "It's not like it's expensive or anything. It probably cost about $20-$30." The investment paid off—Deeb wore it in what he considers the best hand he ever played.

"There were about sixteen players left. I was the first one to act. I had K-K. I opened for $20,000. The blinds were $4,000-$8,000. I had about $200,000. The average stack was about $200,000 or $250,000. I got called by two players, Bruno Fitoussi and Phil."

"The flop came 10-7-3. It looked like a good flop for two kings. I checked, hoping that they'll bluff at it or if they have a small pair, they'll bet it. Bruno Fitoussi bets $60,000. Phil Ivey raised it like $90,000, and I just put all in.

"Bruno had J-10. He laid it down. Phil said, 'I call.' He turned over two 7's for a set. There's nothing I can do. With that board, I have to play that hand. Nobody can get away from that hand with that board, I don't care who it is." The turn came a king.

"I hit the king like a miracle. I would've been out of the tournament. Phil said, 'It must be your lucky shirt.' It's become a famous shirt. I tell you, everywhere I go every day, at least ten people ask me, 'Where's that shirt?' They say, 'Oh, that's a beautiful shirt. Don't listen to him. We love that shirt.'"

THE RAKE

When you get down to sixteen players battling for one of the nine seats at the final table of the World Series of Poker, or any final table in a multi-table tournament, contradictory factors affect strategy. First, there is the matter of surviving. Just get there to give yourself a chance. Then there is the aggressive approach of amassing chips so that when you reach the final table you have a powerful stack that will help you win it all.

In this case, Deeb had a powerful hand he was trying to turn into a powerful stack, so he played it aggressively. The same goes for Ivey. In checking on the flop, Deeb was waiting for someone with, say, a pair of 4's to bluff at the pot, knowing his kings made him more than a 91 percent favorite. Or, if one of his opponents was betting with a 10 in his hand for top pair the way Fituossi was, Deeb was still better than 3-1 to take down the pot.

The reason for these hypothetical examples is to show the process of putting an opponent on a hand based on betting patterns and your knowledge of that opponent's style, and then figuring your odds of winning the pot with your holdings.

When Fituossi bet out and Ivey re-raised, Deeb had the kind of pot he was looking for with his hand, so he moved all in, only to find he was a big underdog. So he happily accepted the miracle king on the turn to beat Ivey.

And he still has the shirt.

Dead money: Derogatory term referring to amateurs entering poker tournaments. So-called dead money players won the World Series of Poker main events in 2002 (Robert Varkonyi), 2003 (Chris Moneymaker), and 2004 (Greg Raymer). **Blinds:** Two forced bets to encourage action in each hand. The small blind is posted by the player to the left of the dealer button. The big blind is posted by the player two seats to the left of the dealer. The amount of the small blind is half the big blind. Other players wishing to participate in the hand must at least match the amount of the big blind. In tournaments, blinds are raised at predetermined intervals, usually every ninety minutes or two hours.

♠♦ MARTIN DE KNIJFF ♥♣

MARTIN DE KNIJFF SAT IN THE LUXURIOUS BELLAGIO HOTEL IN LAS VEGAS IN APRIL 2004, smiling broadly, poised and gracious, winner of more than $2.7 million in the $25,000 buy-in World Poker Tour's Five Star World Poker Classic No Limit Hold'em championship.

The stunning payout made the personable Swede the biggest winner of an open poker tournament in history. For a couple months, anyway. Then **Greg Raymer** walked away with a staggering $5 million in the 2004 World Series of Poker world championship. But in poker, as in life, you take what you can get, and de Knijff (pronounced dek-NAYF) has always taken it fast and large.

He began his card-playing career at thirteen with bridge, and after moving from his native Gothenburg to Stockholm, he became a Life Master at twenty-one. "I won like nine championships for players under twenty-five," the thirty-two-year-old de Knijff says matter-of-factly. During this time, he worked at the Swedish Bridge Federation as a teacher, but he found that most of the action was in poker and backgammon, so he gravitated to the card game.

"Poker is more challenging because you're by yourself," de Knijff says. "Bridge is about partnerships."

While poker may pay some of the bills, de Knijff's true passion is sports betting and handicapping. He also is the face of an Internet poker site, martinspoker.com, and is venturing into publishing.

"I have a poker lifestyle magazine coming out in Sweden," he says. "It will have strategy and analysis for the beginner and people who are interested in poker. One of the best chefs in Sweden will write about food and how he financed his education by playing poker. There will be a lot of reports from tournaments when we go to Monte Carlo, Barcelona, Vienna, Vegas."

De Knijff says the best hand he ever played came in a Pot Limit Omaha cash game at Binion's Horseshoe during the World Series of Poker in 2001 and involved Sam Farha, a past WSOP Pot Limit Omaha bracelet winner.

"We were playing $50-$100 Pot Limit Omaha," de Knijff says. "I'd been running very well. I had almost $70,000. Sammy Farha comes and sits down at the table. He's waiting for a bigger game. There's no seat at the $300-$600 Pot Limit game. So he sits down to play $50-$100, and he has about $200,000 in front of him.

"Now he's going to start raising blind. He's not going to look at his cards. I'm on the button and I didn't have a good hand: A-K-7-3, K-7 of hearts and the blank ace of spades.

"Mansour Matloubi is at the table too. I hadn't seen him for a very long time and he showed up there for the World Series in 2001. He was a little bit stuck in the game. I think he had about $40,000 in front of him. I started with $15,000, so I was about $55,000 ahead. Two guys call, and I decide to call with this crappy hand. Sammy is in the big blind. I know Sammy is going to raise. I figure I'd see what happens."

Indeed, Farha raised without looking at his cards. Matloubi called, as did another player and de Knijff. The flop came K-4-2, two spades. De Knijff had a gutshot straight draw and two spades with the blank ace of spades.

"Now, Sammy checks and Mansour bets the pot. Sammy hasn't looked at his cards. He raised in the dark and now he's checking in the dark. Mansour bets the pot. I play the pot like I have the nut flush draw, so I call, and Sammy calls. Now he looks at his cards and he calls. Now the 7 of spades comes on the turn.

"I have kings and 7's—top two—and the bare ace of spades. Now Sammy checks, Mansour bets the pot again, and I'm pretty sure he has a set. The pot right now is about $16,000, and now I raise to make it $24,000, and then raise $24,000. Sammy now thinks for a long time and he calls. Mansour lays it down.

"I have $38,000 left. The river comes the 9 of spades. There are four spades on the board. Sammy checks and I bet all in.

"He had never played with me before. He stares me down and it feels like forever. At the time, this was a lot of money for me. To make a bluff for $38,000 on the river was a huge bet. I had $70,000 before the pot started. I shouldn't have been in the pot from the beginning. But I'm betting this. Meanwhile, Sammy had four spades in his hand —a 10-high flush. He thinks for a very long time and decides to call.

"I think it was a very good learning experience for me. First of all, now you know how it feels to make a big bluff and not have it work out. You're thinking about what did I do? Did I make a move that he picked up?

"It was very reasonable that I had the nut flush. Why else would I call on the flop? What would I possibly have? And then raising $24,000 on the turn when a spade comes off, what could I possibly have? So I'm playing the pot as if I had a flush draw.

"That was the biggest bluff I ever tried in a cash game. But it showed me I was capable of making these kinds of plays."

Raising blind: To raise without looking at your cards. Also known as raising in the dark. **Blank ace:** In Omaha, where you must use exactly two cards from your hand and exactly three cards from the board, a blank ace refers to holding the ace but no other card of the same suit, thus preventing you from making a flush. **Gutshot:** An inside straight draw in which one card will make the hand. For instance, if you are holding a 2-3-5-6, you need a 4 to complete a straight. Also known as a belly buster. **Check:** To pass on opening the betting on a particular round. **Nut flush:** The best possible flush based on what the board is showing.

THE RAKE

Here's a hard poker truth: You cannot bluff somebody who does not fear losing the amount of money being bet.

For de Knijff, a $38,000 bluff on the river was a big deal. It was everything he had left, and accounted for more than half his stack when the hand started. But for Farha, who sat down with $200,000 in a $50-$100 Pot Limit Omaha Game, it was a pittance to call a player he had never seen before.

The fact is, de Knijff played everything as well as it could be played, if he was going to play a bad hand in the first place. When a spade draw hit the flop, de Knijff knew he held the nut card—the ace of spades—the one card everyone else on a flush draw feared. He also knew that without another spade in his hand, he couldn't make the flush, because in Omaha you must use exactly two cards from your hand and exactly three cards from the board.

However, he could *represent* the flush draw with some aggressive betting and bluff to make less courageous opponents fold. Against any other typical player in that game, de Knijff's move would have worked, and here's the proof: He made Mansour Matloubi lay down what de Knijff believed was a set.

But against a player with a massive stack, de Knijff was bluffing without the vital element of pressuring someone for whom the size of the bet mattered. Still, de Knijff's story serves as a blueprint for what all poker players must go through to become better: realizing he was capable of making such a big play at such a critical time.

♠ ◆ ANNIE DUKE ♥ ♣

ANNIE DUKE IS THE MOTHER OF FOUR BY DAY, AND ONE OF THE toughest poker players in the world by night. The charismatic Poker Mom likes to say that raising children provides her with a loving balance against the harsh competition of poker, and also with the emotional control to excel at both.

After winning her first WSOP bracelet in 2004, Duke captured the $2 million winner-take-all World Series of Poker Tournament of Champions, beating nine other top players, including her older brother, **Howard Lederer**, the brilliant "Professor of Poker."

In one of the most touching moments in televised poker—and one that runs counter to her fierce table image—Duke wept after eliminating the brother she adores and idolizes, the man who taught her how to play big-time poker in the first place.

Duke and Lederer often recount stories of family competition while growing up in New Hampshire. Lederer likes to note how cards and game pieces regularly went flying and how it was not usually he who was doing the flinging. "I was only six!" Duke exclaims, defending herself. Years later, the story goes, Lederer wrote down a list of playable hands on a napkin to begin young Annie's formal poker education. (She also has a few advanced degrees of her own: Duke graduated from Columbia University and was a Ph.D candidate in cognitive psychology at the University of Pennsylvania.)

These days, the forty-year-old Duke is doing plenty of schooling of her own. She's open for discussion on her website, annieduke.com; she was executive producer of a TV pilot based on her life, *All In*; and she has even tutored poker aficionado Ben Affleck, who won the 2004 California State Poker Championship.

Duke says the best hand she ever played came early in the $2 million winner-take-all World Series of Poker Tournament of Champions in 2004.

"I had just tripled up [my chips] and I start the hand with something like $280,000. **Daniel Negreanu** opened in first position for $36,000, and I said to him, 'How much do you have left besides that?' I said that because I had two 10's. He said, 'Another $90,000.' I said, 'I'm raising you all in.'"

After Duke raised the $90,000, action folded around to **Greg Raymer** in the big blind. Raymer went all in, meaning Duke would have to risk the rest of her stack.

"So there's about $450,000 I could win," Duke says. "I'd have to call $150,000. That means I'm getting 3-1 odds. Now here's the interesting situation about being in that spot with two 10's: Raymer obviously has a big hand, because there's a first position raise and a second position re-raise. That's very early in the action, so we're supposed to have big hands with eight people still at the table.

"I know he has a big hand, but if there's any possibility that he has A-K I have to call, because there are more combinations of A-K than there are of, say, aces. If he has A-K, I'm a 6-5 favorite. If he has an overpair, I'm a $4\frac{1}{2}$-1 dog. So if I can't eliminate A-K, I have to call because I'm getting 3-1.

"I sat there for about three minutes. I think ESPN showed the decision for about fifteen seconds. But it took me three minutes. I was apologizing to everybody. I knew that Greg was incredibly happy with the hand from the way he was sitting. But he had a little bit of a tell.

"So the question for me was: Is Greg somebody who would be that comfortable with A-K in his hand in this situation? And I decided no. After three minutes of agony, because the pot was so big, I said no, he would not be comfortable with A-K. And not only that, but I don't think he has jacks or queens. Once I eliminate jacks or queens, I can certainly eliminate A-K with ease, because I can't call against jacks or queens, either. I decided in the end that he was so comfortable with his hand that he had to have aces or kings.

"And I fold, leaving myself crippled with only $150,000, right after I got close to $300,000. It was, 'Finally, I'm healthy,' and literally the very next hand, I'm back to $150,000. Very, very frustrating. That was right before the dinner break.

"A few other players in the tournament said, 'How could you fold?' There's too good a possibility of A-K; you have to call with two 10's there.' But he had kings. I studied it. I really thought about it. I said, 'I'm a $4\frac{1}{2}$-1 dog,' and I folded.

"Now, what's interesting is it was relatively early and there were still eight players left at the table. But it was a situation where I stopped myself from going broke when I know there were some other players at that table that would've put themselves in the situation where, only one in every $5\frac{1}{2}$ times, they would have stayed in the tournament.

"I have to say that that's probably the hand that I'm proudest of and it was a hand where I crippled myself, but I stopped myself from going broke."

Triple up: To go all in and get called by two players, and then win the hand. You end up with three times the chips you started the hand with. **Tell:** A physical or verbal mannerism that gives away the strength or weakness of your hand.

THE RAKE

The first thing to consider in this hand is the structure of the tournament. It was winner-take-all and featured a table of great players: Duke's brother Howard Lederer, World Series Player of the Year Daniel Negreanu, nine-time bracelet winner Phil Hellmuth. And no one at the table was hotter than Greg Raymer, coming off winning $5 million in the 2004 WSOP main event.

In a situation like that, where survival is so critical, you need to have the discipline to lay down a good hand, but only after gathering as much information as possible. When one player calls another all in, everyone else tends to get out of the way. But here, Raymer was coming over the top of Duke's re-raise in a tournament where few were likely to mess around with anything but the nuts or close.

If Raymer held A-K, Duke was a 57 percent favorite to win the hand, so the 3-1 pot odds would be advantageous. But if he had aces or kings, Duke was less than 20 percent to win, meaning she was going to win only one in five times for the same pot that was offering 3-1.

After figuring the math, she was left to determine what kind of hand she was up against. It came down to her physical read of Raymer—that he was sitting confidently, a sign he was holding an overpair. Once Duke determined that, the pot odds and the prospect of going broke told her to fold.

♠ ♦ ANTONIO ESFANDIARI ♥ ♣

ANTONIO ESFANDIARI IS FEARLESS. FEARLESS ENOUGH TO PLAY almost any two cards, and play them as aggressively as any poker player in the world. He believes you have to give action to get it, and he gives it in a good, profitable, and entertaining way.

An ex-professional magician who still carries his bag of tricks to the table, Esfandiari came to big-time poker in his early twenties and is one of the many younger players feared around the world.

The twenty-six-year-old Tehran native did not speak a word of English when he moved with his family to San Jose, California, at the age of nine. He learned magic while in college and fell for poker shortly thereafter.

A showman who flips chips between his fingers with each hand at the table, Esfandiari jolted the World Poker Tour's first season when he took third place in a tournament that earned him $44,000 and prompted him to adopt the "Kid 44" nickname inscribed on his visor. Esfandiari also roared to a win in the L.A. Poker Classic in 2004—pocketing $1,399,135—and after celebrating all night still went on to make the final table of the World Poker Tour Invitational the next day. A former roommate of **Phil "The Unabomber" Laak**, Esfandiari captured his first World Series of Poker bracelet in 2004, winning the $2,000 buy-in Pot Limit Hold'em event.

Esfandiari says the best hand he ever played came during that L.A. Poker Classic win, and, typically, it featured his distinctive style of play.

"It was six-handed. I had about $600,000-$800,000 in chips. The two hands before that, I had raised and they came back over the top. I just had to put a stop to it. Let them know I'm sick."

Esfandiari drew 10-6 of diamonds and continued his aggressive style, this time raising $50,000. Vinny Vinh came back over the top upward of $100,000. "So I raised and he re-raised, and I thought about it and thought about it, and then I moved all in on him with a 10-6 of diamonds. Then he thought about it and thought about it.

"I remember thinking, What do I have to do to make him fold? So I stood up and started walking around, just kind of pacing around the table. A good friend of mine, **Gabe Thaler**, a great player, told me that whenever he gets up and walks around, people always tend to fold their hands. Obviously he feels that it makes people think you have a strong hand. It's kind of a reverse tell.

"I'd never done it before. Final table. Championship event. One-point-four million at stake. I said, I'm going to try it. He sat for a good three, four minutes. So I got up and started walking around. Pacing back and forth. He's looking over at me. And I'm like, Please, for the love of God, fold your cards!"

Finally, Vinh mucked his cards. Vinh held A-2. Esfandiari showed his 10-6 of diamonds. "He went sick. It was such a turning point. I either go from looking like a super-genius, which is the way it worked out, or I look like a super-retard. There's no in-between. It's either retard or genius.

"Now, everybody knows what I did was crazy and they're afraid to play against me. Also, they know I'm always playing garbage, so when I do get a real hand, I seem to get action."

THE RAKE

There are two important lessons here: First, if you are going to sell a bluff, then really sell it, and second, if you give action, you will get action. Esfandiari certainly sold the bluff, resorting to a physical display that is about the only remaining area of deceit at the table because tournament rules prohibit players from making comments about the strength or weakness of their hand if it is aimed at prompting action. In the old days, you could talk a player out of his hand and into poverty. No more.

Next, Esfandiari's willingness to play "crazy" is a prime example of table image. Everybody has one, even if you are not trying to create one. A maniac makes you believe he will play any hand. A calling station is too stubborn to fold and too passive to raise. A tight player bets only the premium hands. Esfandiari's reckless image set him up so that when he actually had a strong hand, opponents called him down. A monster turning point of that tournament was when a player holding A-8 challenged Esfandiari, who had the goods and promptly bested two players with pocket queens. If Esfandiari had any other kind of table image, the player with A-8 probably would not have played. Later, during heads-up play, Vinh thought Esfandiari was trying to make a move, ran into wired aces, and it was all over.

Reverse tell: Faking a physical or verbal mannerism to deceive an opponent into thinking you're strong when you're weak, or vice versa. **Maniac:** A super-aggressive player who seems to be raising every pot from any position with any two cards. A maniac will run over a table unless you play back at him.

♠ ♦ SCOTT FISCHMAN ♥ ♣

YOU GET THE FEELING WATCHING SCOTT FISCHMAN PLAY THAT HE KNEW EARLY ON World Series of Poker bracelets were his destiny. The Pennsylvania-born Fischman moved to South Jersey when he was five, after his father had taken a job as director of entertainment for an Atlantic City casino. Seven years later, it was on to Las Vegas as Fischman's father went to work for another casino.

"A friend of mine named Jordan Salmon got me into poker," Fischman says. "His grandfather, Merrill Hunt, won a World Series bracelet in the '80s. He taught me how to play, and we used to ditch school and go out to the casinos with fake IDs. When I turned twenty-one, I decided I didn't want to go to school anymore. So I needed a job and said, Hell, I might as well deal poker."

Fischman dealt for less than two years at the Mirage, but was playing so much and making enough money that he quit dealing and began playing full-time. Soon after he went pro, Fischman hooked up with similar young aggressive players, including Russ "Dutch" Boyd, Brett Jungblut, Joey Bartholdi, and David Smythe to become The Crew.

"I was really tight, Brett was really loose, Dutch was really intellectual about the game, Joey was kind of a mix," says Fischman, who operates his own poker site, thefishtank.com. "I told those guys about what's important about playing tight. They told me about what's important about playing loose. Yadda, yadda, yadda." Clearly, the strategy worked: In the 2004 World Series of Poker, members of The Crew took three firsts, a second, and a third, cashing fifteen times.

The twenty-four-year-old Fischman says the best hand he ever played came in the $1,500 buy-in No Limit Hold'em event in the 2004 World Series of Poker: "Hands down, it's the most critical hand I've played in my life.

"It was about thirty minutes after I lost about sixty percent of my chips with aces. I was down to about $12,000. The blinds were $800-$1,600, with, I believe, a $300 ante. I'd say there were about forty players left in the tournament.

"I was pretty much cruising before I picked up those aces and had a lot of momentum. Then I kind of went into a mode of playing tight, trying to survive, pick a hand, find a spot. With $12,000 in chips and $800-$1,600 blinds and an ante, you don't have much time to maneuver. I was pretty much looking for any hand.

"**Scotty Nguyen** is at my table with a mountain of chips, and he's raising every hand and playing great. That's his style. I'm pretty much waiting for any hand to play."

Once again, Nguyen raised it to $4,000 from early position. Fischman looked down to find A-J of hearts. "Immediately, I was like, This is it. I'm going all in. There's no way I can fold this hand. I have the blinds coming up in like three hands. I'm about to lose 40 percent of my stack.

"So I'm about to push all my chips in and something stopped me. I have no idea what it was. I thought about it, and my brain was telling me, 'Push all your chips in, push all your chips in, push all your chips in.' And my hand just went into the muck."

"I have no idea to this day what made me fold. I guess it was gut instinct. It was definitely a point in the tournament where I'd have to play this hand 98 percent of the time. I think the main reason why I folded was that Scotty's going to call me 100 percent of the time. There's no way he's going to fold for the re-raise.

"Somebody would come over the top of him for $12,000 or $15,000 just like I had, and he called one guy with A-4 offsuit. He called one guy with K-10. Somebody would come over the top and he would call and just bust them. It was like a pattern. He was on a rush, in a zone—he was killing people."

So Fischman folded the A-J. A player in late position moved in for $30,000 and Nguyen called. "Now at this point, I get to see what would've happened. Scotty Nguyen turns over A-10 offsuit, and I'm like, Oh, my God. I can't believe I folded the A-J. The guy that re-raised him turns over K-9 offsuit. The guy was bluffing Scotty. The guy was thinking he could get Scotty to fold. Like my intuition told me, Scotty was going to call no matter what.

"Boom, a 10 comes out on the flop. I'm just sitting there awestruck, knowing that if I'd pushed my A-J all in, Scotty would've called, 100 percent, and then he would've hit the 10, and I would've been out.

Button: A hockey puck-like disk that says "Dealer." It designates the last player to receive cards and the last player to act after the flop. It is the best position at the table, which is why it rotates clockwise on each deal, ensuring that each player gets the advantage the button provides.

"I've thought about that hand over and over and over and over. Right after that, I doubled up, and boom, boom, boom, from there on, my whole life just changed on that hand."

Changed, indeed, because Fischman went on to win the tournament and collect his first World Series of Poker bracelet.

THE RAKE

Stack sizes represent power in tournaments, and Scotty Nguyen was money-whipping the table, giving a clinic on how to wield a big stack. Now, consider the dire situation that Fischman was in: Down to $12,000 in chips with $800-$1,600 blinds and $300 antes coming up in three hands, meaning he was going to be forced to put nearly half his stack into the pot before the button circled the table. That's why he was looking for some kind of hand to move in with to double up, and the A-J he drew figured to be as good as it got.

So why did he fold? Because he read his opponent perfectly and realized he didn't have the additional advantage of "fold equity." This is a betting factor that is not often stressed, but it is a part of the best players' games. Fold equity is the percentage, no matter how small, that the table will fold to your raise or re-raise and allow you to take the pot right there.

But Fischman realized there was no chance that, with the way Nguyen was playing, he would lay down to any kind of re-raise. Nguyen was raising everything and calling every all in. And busting players. He was also getting cards, but that's part of reading your opponents and the table, too.

What's more, the player behind Fischman who did go all in probably would not have folded to Fischman's re-raise either, because Fischman's stack was such that he might have moved in with anything, and in that situation a K-9 would look good to another short-stacked player.

Three-handed, Fischman would have had the best chance pre-flop to win the pot, but he was less than a 50 percent favorite. Heads-up against Nguyen's A-10, Fischman was a 74-26 favorite, but when you are risking your entire stack, you at least want some additional juice that your raise or re-raise will scare off the rest of the table. Fischman knew he could not count on that, so he waited for a better spot.

♠ ♦ LAYNE FLACK ♥ ♣

GROWING UP IN SOUTH DAKOTA AND MONTANA, LAYNE FLACK DID NOT SEEM A LIKELY candidate to get to Las Vegas. So he brought Las Vegas to Montana. "I went to college for one year," Flack explains. "I had a couple of roommates who were card players, too, so we didn't get much school in. I went back to Montana and started opening up my own games."

As seemed inevitable, in the mid-1990s, Flack joined some friends for a trip to the real Las Vegas. "When I came down here, it was during the Hall of Fame tournaments, and I won [a $1,500 No Limit Hold'em event]," Flack says. "They put bars up around the city after that. They weren't letting me out. I'm here for good."

Flack stuck around the poker circuit and received some mentoring by poker great **Johnny Chan**. He learned well. Since 1999, Flack has gone on to win five World Series of Poker bracelets. A master of a wild and aggressive style that can make him tough to read—and thus feared by opponents—Flack has captured titles in such varied games as Limit Hold'em, Pot Limit Hold'em, No Limit Hold'em, and Omaha High-Low.

But the thirty-six-year-old Flack, whose aggressive act at the table often runs counter to his shy and private demeanor, is probably best known for beating Los Angeles Lakers owner Jerry Buss heads-up in the World Poker Tour's Pro-Celebrity Invitational at the Commerce Casino in 2003. No hard feelings, however, as Buss has since invited Flack to sit in his luxury suite for Lakers games.

These days, there is a different Layne Flack at the table, one who is alcohol-free. Friends intervened to get Flack into a rehab facility for thirty days in the summer of 2004. "It was more of a retreat rehab to get my actions more in line with my intentions, and to take a break," he explains.

"Poker has a lot to do with momentum and confidence. Alcohol certainly gives people a lot of confidence and momentum. But a lot of doors started closing on me. I'm a high-profile player and a lot of opportunities weren't coming to me that probably would have if I was—how would you say?—more bonded.

"I just made up my mind that I separated everything from business and pleasure. There's just no time for pleasure at all. I used to drink at the table and mix my fun with my work. The biggest thing I miss is card rushes. You get a lot of card rushes when you're drinking."

One of those card rushes came during his back-to-back No Limit Hold'em titles at the World Series of Poker in 2002, and a hand he played against Phillip Marmorstein in the $1,500 buy-in event produced what Flack calls the best he ever played.

"We were probably five-handed and I had about $180,000 in chips." Holding pocket 10's, Flack made it $15,000 to go. Marmorstein called. The flop came 10-10-8 with two clubs, giving Flack quad 10's.

"I thought I wasn't going to make any money on the hand because no one could make anything. I got called." The turn came a 4.

"There were two clubs out there. I was hoping an ace or a king or a club came, so he made something that he would bet. I checked it and he checked it." The river came another 4, the 4 of clubs, putting a flush draw up. Flack checked, Marmorstein moved all in and then Flack called.

"He turned over quad 4's. The person who was staking me was my roommate, Ted Forrest. He came walking in the door right at that time and he heard, 'Layne has quads—over quads!' I got to knock a player out and get his chips. I thought everybody was going to fold because nobody was going to have anything.

"In poker, the bigger your hand, the more you can lose. You lose more money with aces than you make with aces usually. You can lose all your chips and you don't win all their chips most of the time. To make a lot of money, your hands have to be very close, or someone has to suck out."

Flack went on to win that event, as well as the $2,000 buy-in No Limit Hold'em tournament, earning him the nickname Back-to-Back Flack.

THE RAKE

Layne Flack got action on this hand—big action—for two reasons: One, he let his opponent take cards to catch a hand, and two, because he is Layne Flack.

What the latter means is that his aggressive nature—his willingness to raise with any two cards, it seems—eventually leads opponents to play back at him. If he had a tight table image, his opponent would be less inclined to chase the pot, figuring Flack had a solid hand or he would not be playing it.

So when Flack raised $15,000, Marmorstein likely viewed it as a pre-emptive move that would take nearly 20 percent of his stack. But Flack's aggressive image and Marmorstein's pocket 4's prompted him to call.

Flack's smartest move came when he checked on the turn. It is not a revolutionary play, but it is vital to getting all of your opponent's chips. Flack checked with the best hand to give Marmorstein a chance to catch up, hoping Marmorstein would get a big card or a club to complete a flush. Additionally, Flack planted the idea that he was weak. When a 4 fell on the river to give Marmorstein quads, he moved all in, presenting an easy call for Flack holding the absolute nuts.

♠♦ ALAN GOEHRING ♥♣

ALAN GOEHRING HAD SPENT SO MUCH TIME IN SECOND PLACE
that he should have been charged rent. The tall, thin New Yorker
has been runner-up in several major tournaments, most
notably the 1999 World Series of Poker championship and the
$3,000 buy-in No Limit Hold'em event at the Bellagio in 2002.
But he finally copped his first major title in 2003 when he won
the World Poker Tour Championship, beating a big-name final
table that included **Doyle Brunson**, Phil Ivey, and Ted Forrest.

One of the keys to Goehring's game is his superb math skill, which
stems from his early days as a broker on Wall Street. Though he considers
himself retired, Goehring is still involved with some stock and bond trading. The analytical abilities he gained as a trader have also made him a fearless player at the tables,
best exemplified during his World Poker Tour Championship run when he knocked out
Layne Flack by playing J-3 and later eliminated Allen Cunningham by playing a 7-3.

Naturally, Goehring says the best hand he ever played came during that World Poker
Tour Championship in 2003. "I had a big chip lead going into the final table. It was five-
handed. The blinds were $15,000-$30,000. I was the first one to act. I made it
$60,000. Doyle Brunson thought I had nothing because sometimes I raise a lot of
hands, so he moved all in for about $500,000. Ted Forrest thought for awhile and ended
up calling."

Holding pocket jacks, Goehring faced a tough decision. An all in followed by a cold
call might have meant at least one player held aces, kings, or queens, which would have
left Goehring a 4-1 underdog.

"I kind of put one on A-Q, the other on pocket 10's. I thought if Ted had kings or
queens, he would've rushed into the pot because he probably wants me to fold. But he
thought about it, so I think you can kind of take him off those hands. And if Doyle had aces,
I think he may not have moved all in and it was probable that I would fold the hand. He
might raise half his chips and then on the flop try to get 100 percent of the pot from there.

"Two jacks, when two people go all in in front of you, 99 percent of the time, you
should fold that hand. People think I'm crazy that I called with two jacks, but I did it
because I didn't think they had aces, kings, and queens.

"The worst for me is I would have been the chip leader and Ted or Doyle would've
been eliminated. And if Ted or Doyle won the hand, he would've been in second place."
The flop came three low cards. The turn was also a low card, putting a straight draw on
the board. If a 4 came on the river, it would've created a straight to the 6 and a three-
way split. "I just needed no ace or no queen because Doyle had Q-8 and Ted had A-J.

Neither Brunson nor Forrest got his card, and Goehring was on his way to his first major tournament victory and a $1,011,886 payday. "It was my greatest hand because it knocked out the legendary Doyle Brunson and Ted Forrest, who's also a great player, at the same time."

THE RAKE

People who watched this hand thought everyone had misplayed it. Some observers believed that with a dicey hand such as pocket jacks, Goehring should have raised more to represent a bigger hand. Others thought Brunson should never have moved all in with such marginal holdings as Q-8. Still others question Ted Forrest's play with A-J because that's a dangerous hand to call with when someone has moved in ahead of you. And still others contend that Goehring had no business calling with two jacks after an all in and a cold call behind it.

The thing is, you generally find one of two environments at a final table: extremely tight play, with lots of folding and surrendering of blinds, or the kind of extremely loose play where even legends move in with Q-8.

Given the loose play at this table—players were going all in every five hands or so without waiting for pocket aces or kings—Goehring had great instincts to believe his jacks carried more power than usual. In fact, he was slightly better than 50-50 pre-flop to beat Brunson and Forrest. By the turn, he was almost 70 percent to win the hand.

And there is another thing to consider: Stack sizes matter at a final table, and in considering whether to call in that situation, Goehring knew he would still be the chip leader no matter what happened, while whoever won the hand would be second. So with that type of advantage, Goehring seized the chance to get a mountain of chips and eliminate half of his remaining four opponents.

♠ ♦   PHIL GORDON   ♥ ♣

PHIL GORDON KNOWS HOW TO LIVE LARGE, AND NOT JUST BECAUSE HE'S 6'9". A FORMER teenage prodigy, the El Paso-native graduated from Georgia Tech at the age of twenty with a degree in computer science. He became a software engineer at Netsys Technologies, Inc., before it was purchased by Cisco Systems for $95 million in cash and stock.

"I got rich enough for a twenty-six-year-old, rich enough that I felt I could quit my job and never work again," Gordon says plainly. "It's not crazy money, but I didn't have to take any more stuff from anyone, and I didn't."

What Gordon did was take off on a world tour. He donated almost all of his worldly possessions to Goodwill, stuffed a backpack with basic necessities, and for the next five years traveled to nearly fifty countries on six continents.

Now thirty-five, Gordon still looks back on those adventures with great fondness, such as the day he agreed to climb Mount Kilimanjaro. "I didn't think I could do it," he recalls. "I was in Zanzibar, drinking in a bar by myself, and this girl walked up and we started chatting. Three hours later, she says, 'Hey, what are you doing next?' I say, 'I don't know. What are you doing next?' She says, 'Well, I'm going to climb Mount Kilimanjaro.' I say, 'God, that's exactly what I was about to do.' That's how I got conned into doing that."

He also went diving with great white sharks, swam in the Great Barrier Reef, and even judged a wet T-shirt contest in the middle of the Australian Outback. "The girls weren't so good," Gordon laments. "It was the middle of the Outback, after all."

Upon returning to the United States, Gordon began his poker career in earnest. And although he has written his own strategy book, *Poker: The Real Deal*, and co-hosted *Celebrity Poker Showdown* on Bravo for the past two years, he has never lost his wanderlust. In 2003, he bought a huge RV with his best friend, poker pro Rafe Furst, and the two began their self-proclaimed "Greatest Road Trip in Sports History." Starting at the Super Bowl in San Diego, they hit more than 140 sporting events in forty states while raising $100,000 for the Cancer Research and Prevention Foundation.

Gordon says the best hand he ever played came during the main event of the 2001 World Series of Poker and involved his "archenemy," 1989 World Series of Poker champion Phil Hellmuth.

"There were fourteen people left. I was the chip leader at the table with $680,000 and Phil had $640,000. I was in middle position and I had pocket kings.

"Mike Matusow, who's a well-known pro, tight-aggressive player, is under the gun.

There are only seven people at the table, so it's a short table, as well.

"The blinds were $6,000 and $12,000, and Mike made it $30,000 to go. Anyone who raises from under the gun has a premium hand. People aren't screwing around under the gun because you have six more people to act behind you. Mike had about $350,000. Everybody knows he's got a decent hand.

"The only hand that can beat me is aces. So I have to raise here and I have to find the right amount. I want him to call with queens, but I want him to re-raise with aces so I can throw my hand away. And I want him to call with A-K. I want *him* to make a decision, and I should be able to tell what he has based on the way he plays the hand. If he re-raises all in, I'm thinking about calling.

Under the gun: The first player to act in a hand. **Capped:** The maximum number of raises on each round.

"I raised it to $100,000. Now, $100,000 is a huge amount of chips at this point. A huge amount. And he knows that I know that he raised under the gun, so I've got to have a huge hand here—aces, kings, or A-K. I can't be doing this with any other hand."

The action folds around to Hellmuth in the small blind. After seeing the pot get raised to $30,000 under the gun and then re-raised to $100,000, Hellmuth moves all in for $640,000.

"He knows Mike has a very good hand, and he knows that *I* know Mike has a good hand, and yet I still want to raise Matusow, so I have to have a monster hand. He's re-raising this.

"This is where you delve into a guy's psychology. Phil wants to get to the final table of the World Series of Poker more than any human being on the planet. He's seen it go raise, re-raise, and yet I have him covered. The only hand he can have is aces. He can't do that with kings. He has *got* to have pocket aces, period, end of story. He's got to.

"So Mike Matusow sits back in his chair and he can't believe it. He picks up his pocket queens and puts them above his head so the audience can see behind him. Now I know he's got pocket queens. It gets to me. I think for about a minute. I know I'm going to fold, but you want to make sure you're going to fold pocket kings before the flop. It's a big thing to do.

"I said, 'Phil, I know you have the best hand,' and I tossed my cards in front of me. He turns over his pocket aces. I said, 'Everybody knows you had that.'

"He said, 'What did you fold, A-Q offsuit?'

"I said, 'Yeah. That's what I had.'

"He said, 'That's what I put you on.'

"I said, 'Come on, dude. You think I'm screwing around? I had pocket kings!'

"He said, 'You did *not*,' and he stands up from his chair and says, 'You did *not* fold pocket kings before the flop. No way!'

"I reached over and turned my hand over. He was crazy because he'd won only $130,000 in a pot where he had aces against pocket queens and kings.

"The whole thing is keeping yourself in action in a tournament."

THE RAKE

You have to gain information about the strength or weakness of your hand wherever you can find it. Start by evaluating your opponent's bet and personality. Is he a wild player given to erratic betting with suspect hands, or do you give him credit for having game? Is he playing because he likes action or because he is on a manic quest for a tournament win?

The biggest factor generally is the betting pattern. Hellmuth's re-raise after a bet under the gun and a significant raise from middle position told Gordon there was a hand that could beat his kings, as tough a hand to lay down as there might be. But if Gordon's read on Hellmuth's and Matusow's hand was right—and it was—his chances of winning the hand were less than 20 percent.

What's more, Hellmuth's personality, in this case his outsized thirst for another main event bracelet, married so convincingly with Gordon's read on the hand that it screamed "fold." A key dynamic here is that Gordon's move came in a no-limit tournament, not in a limit game. If this were a limit game like the kind people play at home, each street likely would be capped because limit is a big-card game and each player knows he could go broke and still reach into his pocket for more money. Not so in a tournament. You go broke, you go home. The key to tournament play is surviving. And the key to surviving is having the discipline to lay down big hands. So know who your opponent is and know why he's playing. Remember, poker is not about cards and chips, it's about people.

♠ ♦ GAVIN GRIFFIN ♥ ♣

IT IS LATE SUMMER 2004 AND GAVIN GRIFFIN IS DRIVING ACROSS THE southeastern United States, leaving a family vacation in Florida. Griffin is returning for classes at Texas Christian University in Fort Worth, Texas, where he is working on a degree in speech pathology, and he is joking into his cell phone, "I want to have something to fall back on if this poker thing doesn't work out."

Griffin's "poker thing" certainly looked like it was working out. The then-twenty-two-year-old Darien, Illinois, native had just copped $270,420 for winning the $3,000 buy-in Pot Limit Hold'em event at the 2004 World Series of Poker, becoming the youngest bracelet winner in history. If nothing else, he had books and tuition covered.

Griffin began his poker education playing in $2-$4 and $3-$6 games with college friends around Fort Worth, Dallas and Arlington. In 2003, he and his college friends went to Phoenix to play $20-$40, games and, upon finishing school, he started dealing at a casino in East Chicago, Indiana.

"While I was dealing, I was kind of like a semipro, just trying to get a bankroll started," he says. "In January [2004], I went on the Poker Stars cruise. That's basically when I started playing strictly for winning. Most dealers don't translate what they see very well. It seems like most dealers pick up bad habits from players. Because I'd already had a pretty firm background, I didn't have that problem."

From Phoenix, Griffin hit Las Vegas for the first time to see just how good his game was. Pretty damn good, it turns out. "Before I left for Vegas, I was in Fort Worth for about a month, hanging out with my girlfriend and playing the rest of the time I was awake," Griffin recalls. "Before I left for Vegas, I told my friends that I was going to become the youngest bracelet winner ever. I was just joking around with them. But it actually worked out that way."

Naturally, Griffin says the best hand he ever played came during his bracelet-winning event when he pulled off a stone-cold bluff in three-handed play against **Gabe Thaler** and Gary Bush.

"I had 8-9, Gary had J-8, and Gabe had 7-6," Griffin recalls. "I limped on the button, Gabe limped in the small blind and Gary checked.

"I had really been pounding those two guys to death since we got to three-handed. I had been really aggressive since we got to the final table because I came in with the chip lead and had built it up. I had almost a third of the chips in play when we got to the final table. By the time we got to three-handed, I had been raising so much that when I limped, I hadn't intended to throw them off that much. I just didn't really want to get involved in a big pot with 8-9. I'd rather see a flop really cheap with that hand.

"When Gary made that comment—'That's the first time you've done that [limped from the button]'—and went crazy about it, I changed my thinking in the hand right then. I had literally raised probably 98 percent of the hands that I was on the button. I was raising almost every pot. And if I wasn't raising, I was folding. That was the first time during the two and a half or three hours that we played three-handed that I limped in. That's what really messed Gary up at first.

"When he made that comment, I made the decision to play the hand a little different-ly than I intended to. I was intending to see if I could flop a big hand and bluff some-body. I knew that anything that flopped, they were going to put me on a big hand, no matter what. When he said that, I decided that if they're going to put me on a big hand, I might as well play it like a big hand."

The flop came A-K-6, indeed creating the potential for a big hand. "If I had limped with aces or kings or A-K in that position and that flop came down, I would check the flop, no matter what. When Gabe checked and Gary checked, I checked behind to keep up the image of me having a big hand."

Limp: To call the minimum bet. **Drawing dead:** To have lost the hand even with a card or two to come.

The turn came a jack, and Bush and Thaler checked. "It felt to me like they were giv-ing me the pot at that point. Even if that whole reaction hadn't happened, at that point, if they're going to check to me twice, I'm going to take a stab at the pot anyway.

"It was a $48,000 pot. I bet about $37,000. Gary said, 'I can't figure out what he limped with.' Gabe said, 'He's either got nothing or the nuts.' Then Gabe folded, and Gary showed me a jack after he agonized over it for awhile. I tried not to look at it because I didn't want to give off any sort of reaction. He had me destroyed. I'm drawing dead at that point once I saw he had a jack. I tried not to look to give anything away because I know that's why he showed it to me.

"It was the most high-profile hand I've played. Everybody who says, 'I watched the show,' they all say that bluff with 8-9 was great, one of the best hands they'd seen."

THE RAKE

There is a reason a lot of players don't talk much at the table: They might be giving away information. In this case, Gary Bush gave away his belief that Gavin Griffin was making a play by limping on the button when he had been so aggressive to that point. What Griffin did with that information was brilliant. He completely changed his approach to the hand, and if Bush thought he was making a play, well, then Griffin would make one. It's one thing to call an audible in your play when you first look at your cards. It's scary good when you can do it in the middle of a hand.

Particularly in Hold'em, it's not necessarily what you have, it's more what you can represent. Bush couldn't put Griffin on a hand, so he had to give him credit for having a big one, and here's why: First, Griffin came out with a different betting pattern, even if he hadn't realized how different it looked to his opponents. Second—and this is the key to pulling off a bluff—Griffin proceeded to bet the big hand he was representing the way he had previously bet the big hands he actually had. Third, when Griffin bet on the turn, he chose an amount—$37,000 into a $48,000 pot—that looked like he was begging for a call. Griffin's opponent read the transparent-looking underbet exactly as Griffin had hoped, and Griffin got the fold he wanted.

♠♦ HASSAN HABIB ♥♣

THERE IS A RUMOR THAT HASSAN HABIB ONCE SMILED AT THE POKER TABLE.
It was believed to be in 2004, right around the time he beat 212 other players to win
the Seven Card Stud Hi/Lo Eight Or Better tournament at the World Series of Poker
to grab his first gold bracelet. But confirmation that the man behind the signature
brown-tinted, half-wrap sunglasses cracked so much as a smirk remains under
investigation.

It's not just the fact that Habib seemingly has no muscles in his face. It is his ability to play aggressively, play conservatively, play differently—sometimes all in the
same round—and to do it with a Botox-worthy serenity that makes him a feared and
respected poker player.

Born in Karachi, Pakistan, in 1962, Habib was a top teenage tennis player before
moving to the United States in 1980, where he found a world of difference. "It's a lot
more liberal over here and there is less obligation," Habib says. "Everything's based
on religion in Pakistan, but over here there's a separation of state and religion. I
really enjoy that."

Habib attended the University of Redlands in California, where he studied business and minored in psychology. "It probably helps me out a little bit in poker," he
says. "I played a little bit when I was in college at Redlands when I went to Vegas a
couple of times."

For five years after college, Habib ran several video stores. But as his poker playing
grew, he began to win small tournaments. Finally, in 1996, Habib sold his video business and devoted himself to poker full-time. Good call. Because in 2000,
Habib played his way to the final tables of the World Series of Poker
world championship (finishing fourth and collecting $326,000),
the Tournament of Champions, *and* the World Poker Open.

In 2004, Habib not only made the final table, he was one
of the final two players in the World Poker Tour
Championship. In the $25,000 buy-in event that at the time
was the biggest tournament in poker history, Habib eventually got ousted by **Martin de Knijff**, but a runner-up check for
more than $1.3 million can be a lovely parting gift.

While the money was better in 2004, Habib cites the 2000 World
Series of Poker main event as the best hand he ever played: "It was the
first $10,000 event I ever played. I'm one of the chip leaders on Day Three. I'd been
the chip leader all day long and I lost a few chips, but now the chip leader is at my
table. He's been playing fast and he raises."

Habib had 10-Q offsuit. The flop came 10-J-2, giving Habib second pair. He checked, his opponent made a big bet, and then Habib check-raised. His opponent moved all in.

"Now I'm in great position, but I have to make a judgment call. So I sweated him out for a long time, maybe three, four minutes, and I believed that he was out of line. So I called for all my chips. I was in the top five in chips and I risked all of my chips, on a second pair on three bets.

"And I was right. I had the best hand. And it held up. He had A-Q, so he had a gut-shot straight draw. He needed a king or an ace. The turn and the river were no help to anybody. The pot was worth about $300,000, and I went on to finish fourth that year. That took me to my biggest score ever in a tournament—$326,000."

THE RAKE

Every big-time player will tell you that calling in a tournament is a difficult way to go. Believing the poker gods reward aggressive play, many of the best players favor the fold or raise approach, and here's why:

When you call, you are not in control of the table—or at least that hand—because you are responding to an opponent's move instead of the other way around. What's more, by calling you are not putting pressure on your opponents, and so you are not presenting the opportunity for your opponents to fold.

Players who win are usually the ones who are betting out or raising, even if they are bluffing, because bluffing at least gives you a chance to make your opponent lay down a hand. But sometimes you will have to face the big call—the one for all your chips—the way Habib did. And even then, he attempted to avoid it by checking to feel out his opponent.

Facing an opponent who was playing fast, Habib handled it in the best possible way if he was going to define his hand and learn something about his opponent's. By checking, he forced his opponent to act, which allowed Habib to gain some information. By check-raising, Habib played back at his aggressive opponent, which is the way you need to play against someone who is so active. Aggressive players rarely like being on the receiving end of aggressive play, which can often lead to a fold (you win the pot right there), a call (you can take control of the hand), or coming over the top with a re-raise all in (you have to decide how much of the move is macho posturing and how much is a legitimate hand).

Habib's ability to read his opponent's uncomfortable body language and his instinct about the way his opponent had been playing so fast led him to believe his opponent was making a play. But even if Habib was right, he still could have folded and would have had a lot of chips left. This leads to the ever-contradictory struggle in

Final table: Poker's equivalent of the playoffs. This is where the big payoffs are because this is where the tournament is won. In the World Series of Poker, the final table consists of nine players. In the World Poker Tour events, the final table consists of six players. **Playing fast:** Aggressively betting and raising pots. **Check-raise:** An aggressive move where a player first checks, then waits for an opponent to bet, and when it becomes his turn to act again, he raises **Position:** Your spot in the betting rotation as determined by the dealer button, which moves clockwise on each hand. The later your position, the better. **Second pair:** Pairing the middle card in the flop with the hole card; also known as middle pair. **Betting out:** To lead the betting.

the early and middle stages of a tournament in which you are trying to balance the survival instinct against the need to accumulate chips.

Here's a hard poker truth: No book, no expert, no top pro can give you one incontrovertible rule about that, because the only incontrovertible answer in poker is, "It depends"—it depends on trusting your read on an opponent based on body language, betting pattern, position in the hand, and your history with that person.

♠ ♦ GUS HANSEN ♥ ♣

ANY TWO CARDS CAN WIN. THAT'S THE MOTTON OF THE MANIAC POKER PLAYER, AND IT seems as if Gus Hansen is on a personal crusade to make sure that any two cards, in fact, do win.

The wildly aggressive and wonderfully entertaining native of Copenhagen captivated poker's growing TV audience with his audacity in the first few seasons of the World Poker Tour. Bluffing out top players while holding rags such as 2-4 offsuit, the former bookie and newspaper delivery boy won the L.A. Poker Classic and the Five Diamonds World Poker Classic in the WPT's first season. The next year was even more profitable for Hansen, who won two more WPT events while taking third and sixth in two others.

The thirty-two-year-old Hansen, who has a shaved head and piercing eyes, has been characterized as reckless and called lucky by opponents, and that's fine by him. Because the man knows the math. And amid the chip-rattling, as he plots his next surprising move, he is actually calculating the odds of every possible play.

A longtime games junkie, Hansen's talent for figuring value and equity comes from his legendary backgammon days that included a championship in his native Denmark. Hansen believes his backgammon training gives him the ability to analyze situations more objectively than most poker players.

Typically, Hansen says the best hand he ever played is one that nobody could believe he played—the one against **Antonio Esfandiari** during the World Poker Tour's Bad Boys of Poker event at the Bellagio.

"There were five players left," Hansen says." Antonio, a very aggressive player, raises. I have the 10-8 of diamonds, which is a reasonable, playable hand. I could play it three ways: just fold it and see if you can get a better hand next time; it's reasonable to call; and it's reasonable to raise and try to buy it right there.

"Since he's very aggressive and I know he's capable of laying down hands, I decided to re-raise. He raised to about $30,000, and I made it $130,000. I looked at him, and he was studying for a long, long time, which made me pretty confident that he didn't have a strong hand. Sometimes people think when they have a super-strong hand. I felt pretty sure he had a medium-type hand. After awhile, he decides to move all in for about $400,000.

"Everybody in the world pretty much, I think, would've laid it down. But given the fact that I felt I got a read on him where it was very likely he had a hand like a small pair—5's or 6's—or even a suited ace, I just felt if he had one of those hands, it would be a big mistake for me to fold my 10-8. I felt I had a good read on him and that it was mathematically correct to call. Then he turned over two 7's. You can always second-guess yourself, but I definitely made the right call."

The flop came with an 8, pairing Hansen and leaving Esfandiari gasping for a 7 to stay alive. It never came.

"He was stunned because before I called, **Phil Laak** was at the table, and I said, 'Well, I only have 10-high,' and Phil said, 'Oh, you have two 10's,' because nobody could imagine that I was considering calling with 10-high.

"People, I think, have a little skewed sense of what the different hands are worth. Once they have an ace in their hand, they think it's such a big hand. But the math works a little different. In general, I have a good handle on the math, and if you add in a good read on the guy, it turned out right."

THE RAKE

The big-card mentality that pervades poker got knee-capped by the math here, even though you might never expect it, and here's how: Esfandiari's 7's were about a 52-48 favorite over Hansen's 10-8. By the time Esfandiari had called Hansen's re-raise and then came over the top with a $330,000 all in, Hansen was facing a call of $330,000 to win $620,000, about 50 percent, which is close to the percentage underdog Hansen was. Despite what you think of playing 10-8, Hansen was getting a good price to call with two overcards in this situation.

Rags: Low or bad cards that don't make a good hand. **Suited:** Hole cards of the same suit.

Folding to Esfandiari's re-raise all in still would have left Hansen with a playable number of chips, but stack sizes and the special circumstances of the tournament dictated making the call. The event was winner-take-all. Second place paid nothing. Had there been payouts for lower finishes, Hansen would have faced an extremely tough call.

But that particular situation, plus the fact that Hansen and Esfandiari were the chip leaders, presented Hansen with a chance to crush his nearest competitor and take a commanding chip lead. Certain tournament setups demand big moves.

You need to adjust your playing style to the structure of the particular game. Sometimes you will face quickly increasing blinds that don't allow for a patient, disciplined approach. Sometimes you will play at six-handed tables instead of the customary nine that will force more aggressive play more often.

♠♦ JENNIFER HARMAN ♥♣

JENNIFER HARMAN IS OFTEN REGARDED AS THE BEST WOMAN POKER PLAYER on the planet. But that's not fair, says poker pro **Daniel Negreanu**, who considers her one of the best poker players in the world, period.

"I've been playing poker since I was eight," says Harman, who tells stories of watching her father play and, when he was down, him letting her take over his hand to get him even.

Harman continued to play while pursuing a biology degree at the University of Nevada, Reno, and after finishing her cocktail waitress shifts in a casino poker room in Reno. "Then I went to L.A., and they legalized Hold'em and Stud," Harman says. "They said, 'You should go down there and play,' and I did, and I just said, 'I'm home.' That was it. I've been playing poker professionally for fifteen years."

Married to star hairdresser Marco Traniello, Harman plays regularly at the World Series of Poker and the World Poker Tour events. However, she was unable to play in the 2004 World Series of Poker main event because she needed a kidney transplant. The kidney she now carries came from a niece, and the ordeal moved Harman to put together the Jen Harman Challenge as a way to raise awareness about the importance of organ donation.

Back in action, Harman also antes up in the biggest cash games at the Bellagio and is said to have taken down the largest pot in history—$1.7 million—in a cash game at a major casino at the time. Like every great player, Harman has a terrific grasp of math and figuring the odds in a hand, but she also has the great poker player's ability to read people. If you want to know how impressive Harman's all-around poker abilities are, consider this: **Doyle Brunson** invited her to write the chapter on Limit Hold'em for his long-awaited sequel *Super/System 2*.

A winner of two World Series of Poker bracelets, Harman captured the Deuce-to-Seven No Limit Draw event in 2000, overcoming a huge chip deficit in heads-up play against **Lyle Berman**. What's more, she did it in a game she had never played before.

But then, Harman has a history of pulling off some impressive wins in those kinds of situations, as she details in the best hand she ever played: "It was at the Bellagio. The first time I ever played Pot Limit Omaha in my life. The blinds were $500-$1,000. Cash game with a $100,000 cap.

"I came in raising $2,500. I was holding A-A-Q-3 with ace-high spades. It got re-raised, and the pot grew to $25,000. Doyle Brunson raised the pot, calling the $25,000 and raising it $50,000, so he capped it at $100,000."

Two players folded. Harman called. The flop came 5-6-7 with two clubs. The turn came a 5, and the river came the jack of clubs.

"It was capped on every street. Nobody wanted to turn over their hands. **Chip Jett** said to Doyle, 'Your aces are good, Doyle,' and Doyle said, 'I don't got the aces. Jennifer, turn over your aces.'

"That was the biggest pot I had ever won at the time. It was over $300,000. My hands were shaking. Lyle Berman said, 'I think that was the biggest pot you've ever won in your life.' I couldn't talk."

THE RAKE

Pot Limit Omaha is played more widely in Europe than in the United States, where No Limit Hold'em is the favored choice, but Pot Limit Omaha is gaining popularity in America as players take to the artistry involved.

Like No Limit Hold'em, Pot Limit Omaha—or Pot Limit Anything, for that matter—is a game of wild swings and huge jumps that test your heart and your stack. It does not take long to get from the $500 small blind that Harman, Brunson, and friends were playing to the seemingly unreachable cap of $100,000. But remember, every bet in Pot Limit increases the amount in the pot, which then increases the maximum of each raise. Raise the size of the pot and you have doubled it. So when Brunson called a $25,000 bet, he made the pot worth $50,000, and when he raised the pot, he made it $100,000. Capped. Just like that.

It's likely that Brunson was counting on the quick and wild swings of Pot Limit Omaha to shake Harman's confidence in a game she had never played. Brunson probably figured that the only hand Harman was likely to have to withstand such money-whipping was aces. He was able to put her on a hand, which is one of the most important abilities a poker player must possess. You have to be able to act on your opponent's hand, as well as on your own holdings.

At that point, Brunson tried to run her out of the pot with his typically aggressive betting, and in Pot Limit games, that aggressiveness dumps tremendous pressure on the next player to act, the same way it does in No Limit Hold'em. But Harman stuck it out, knowing a good hand when she held one, even if she had never held one in Pot Limit Omaha before.

♠♦ DAN HARRINGTON ♥♣

IF YOU WANT TO SPOT DAN HARRINGTON PLAYING POKER, JUST LOOK FOR the guy in the green Boston Red Sox hat.

With a lot of chips. At the final table.

In fact, the fifty-nine-year-old Harrington (who heads up Anchor Loans, a mortgage company, in his day job) pulled off one of the greatest recent accomplishments in poker when he sidestepped the landmines of newbies, Internet players, and dangerous professionals populating the two biggest fields in history to make the final tables of the 2003 *and* 2004 World Series of Poker main events.

Born in Boston—hey, it wasn't like he just *found* that Sox cap — Harrington graduated from Suffolk University with a law degree and began practicing real estate and bankruptcy law immediately after school. Like most people, he started playing poker in regular home games, but he made his name as a backgammon star, winning the World Cup of backgammon in Washington, D.C., in 1980.

With some prodding from friends, he ventured to Las Vegas to try his luck at the World Series of Poker. "For the first two years, I played in small side games," Harrington explains. "I learned the craft. Gradually I got really good at it. I started playing side-action games against the best players in the world. I didn't play in tournaments.

"Then tournaments started coming on, and finally, in 1987, I broke down and played in my first major tournament, which was the World Series of Poker main event, because I won a satellite. I came in sixth and I was hooked."

Hooked, indeed, and not satisfied with a mere top-ten finish. In 1995, Harrington won the World Series of Poker main event, and it is the final deal of that tournament against Howard Goldfarb that he cites as the best hand he ever played—one that also serves to show how misleading poker broadcasts can be.

"This is a perfect illustration of where you see a hand on television and they're really explaining the two cards in front of you, and that's the hand. That's only one of about six or seven elements that constitutes a hand.

"You probably have to go back to the last few hours of play. I was up against Howard Goldfarb, and I made him lay down hands in four or five different situations. So I knew he was ready to make a stand. Psychologically, he had to make a stand."

Playing heads-up, Harrington had about $1.9 million, compared to Goldfarb's stack of about $700,000. From the button, Goldfarb made it $120,000 to go. In the big blind, Harrington held 9-8 of diamonds. "I said, This is the hand that could end the tournament. Suited connectors. I liked it. So I called."

The flop came 8-2-6, with two clubs, giving Harrington a pair of 8's. He checked to Goldfarb. "He put his $600,000 out there. Just shoved it into the center. I had to restrain myself from beating him to the center of the pot because I knew without a doubt I had the best hand at that point. I did wait a second for courtesy's sake before I called him.

"Sure enough, he had A-7, unsuited. The turn and river came Q-Q. And I won. I knew it would come to that situation. But let's not underestimate the luck factor, too. Getting lucky makes up for a lot of bungles, believe me. You can look like a genius when you get lucky."

THE RAKE

Harrington admits he had some luck, and truth be told, nobody wins a tournament without it. More important, he was able to read his opponent correctly—not his facial tics or some of the more obvious Hollywood tells, but his mental state.

Harrington *knew* that Goldfarb's frustration was building. Sometimes it comes from just a couple of hands earlier; sometimes it's hours or even days before. This is where television's influence on poker has created some bad habits for newer players. While the proliferation of broadcast poker has taught the game to millions by offering what is essentially a speed-reading course on strategy, TV's collapsed editing process hides the context in which certain moves are made. The cameras also regularly ignore the importance of the discipline of folding because folding just isn't good television. The bottom line is, don't believe everything you see, because you're not seeing everything.

It is one thing to know when an opponent is making a play out of frustration and not because it is mathematically correct. It is quite another to be able to make the play yourself. Harrington knew he had made Goldfarb lay down some good hands and that Goldfarb would try to do the same to him. And Harrington was ready to leverage his psychological advantage.

Side-action games: Another name for cash games that take place while a tournament is going on. **Satellite:** A way to win entry into a tournament. Satellites have reduced entry fees, but the catch is you have to win a single-table or multi-table tournament to gain a spot in the bigger event. **Suited connectors:** Consecutive cards of the same suit.

First, instead of making a bet after he flopped a pair of 8's to find out where he was in the hand, Harrington checked, and here's why: He knew that Goldfarb would make what is known as a continuation bet. Goldfarb had raised before the flop and Harrington expected him to come out firing again. By checking, Harrington gave Goldfarb the impression that he was weak and that Goldfarb could make the big bet that could take down the pot.

In fact, Harrington was about a 4-1 favorite after the flop with his pair against one overcard with two cards left to come, and when Goldfarb moved all in, Harrington quickly called with the best hand and it held up.

♠♦ BOBBY HOFF ♥♣

DESPITE HIS COURTLY MANNER AT THE POKER TABLE, SIXTY-FIVE-YEAR-OLD BOBBY Hoff serves as a bridge to some of the game's colorful outlaw past. "When I was at the University of Texas, I got seriously involved in poker," Hoff recalls. "I had a golf scholarship in 1959. But once I started playing poker, I never made it to a class or the golf course. Second semester I was on my way home, but I had won so much money that I thought I was a great poker player.

"Then I came back home to Victoria, a little town in south Texas. It was a wide-open gambling town. It had three full-fledged casinos in the '60s. One was really a fancy joint—poker around the clock. So I started playing Hold'em and it took me a little while, but I got broke."

Hoff then turned to dealing, taking his daily tips to the poker tables, where "I would play until I was either broke or it was time to go back to work. I slept pretty good a lot of times." As Hoff's game improved, he eventually got himself to Las Vegas. He soon became a dangerous man at the table, and a bigger danger to himself away from it—with serious drug, alcohol, and debt problems. As he once recalled for the book *The Championship Table,* Hoff would regularly cut two lines of cocaine on his nightstand the evening before a game, then carefully cover them with an empty ashtray so the humidity would not ruin them when he went to snort them first thing the next morning.

With the help of friends, and some discipline and pride of his own, Hoff ultimately kicked his destructive habits. The Long Beach, California, native not only continues to play these days, but has also taken to mentoring the talented young player **Gabe Thaler.**

Over the course of his career, Hoff reached the final table of the World Series of Poker world championship event in 1979, suffering some horrendous beats at the hands of amateur Hal Fowler. The final hand alone tells the story: Hoff had pocket aces cracked by an opponent who called a pre-flop raise with 7-6 offsuit—maybe the only player at the final table who would do that—and ended up hitting a gutshot straight.

"In 1979 when I came in second, when I started the tournament, I thought I was play-ing for the money. But when I came down with a real chance to win it, I realized I would've given all the money to win it and get the bracelet," Hoff says. "But I no longer feel that way. Now I wouldn't be moved by the bracelet. The bracelet wouldn't mean anything to me. It's the cash. It's different now. It's probably going to be a non-poker player who's going to win the tournament. They're like the Chinese army. There's thousands of them. It's more like winning the lotto now. It's no longer any way to iden-tify anyone as a great No Limit Hold'em player." On the other hand, Hoff's long view of poker and life might be summed up best this way: "You can't lose playing with bad play-ers."

Hoff says the best hand he ever played came during a cash game more than three decades ago."I was playing in a town way out in the sticks outside Nashville in the early '70s. Poker was played everywhere, and this was a clandestine casino in a town with one general store, one motel, and this poker game in a cinderblock building in the middle of nowhere. There were no windows, just a room. And no security outside, either. I was scared to leave. I had a friend who played in the game, but I was broke, so my friend staked me to play. But he left me there and he went back to the hotel while I played in this game. I was a little uncomfortable. But I played this pot where I had an ace and trey in No Limit Hold'em, and we were playing with cash.

"I had $14,000 in $20 bills. The big blind was like $20, which was a decent-sized game. They said they were farmers, but they must have been farming $20 bills because they had sacks full of twenties. Anyway, in this pot, a very aggressive player was dealing. I mean, literally dealing the way each player did in those days. Mac Fisher was his name. And he didn't raise this pot. Several players limped in and he didn't raise, and I mean he had raised on his deal maybe fifteen times in a row. So I was pretty sure he didn't have very much of a hand. I'm the big blind and I have A-3."

Trey: Another name for a 3. **Overbet:** To make a bet more than the total amount in the pot. **Drawing hands:** Holding cards that could potentially make a straight or a flush, but haven't yet.

The flop came Q-4-3. Action checked all the way around to Fisher, who bet $200. Hoff called. "I'm sure he doesn't have three queens. He probably doesn't have two 4's in his hand because he would've raised with those. And he doesn't have a pair of aces, either.

"The next card came a queen. That put the fourth suit on the board. I checked it to him, and he made a pretty big bet. He overbet the pot. I'm pretty sure he doesn't have a queen and a jack because he didn't raise on his deal. So I called it again."

The river came a jack, and Hoff checked. Fisher bet $3,500, and Hoff thought for a while and called. "Now, the guy who drove me up to the game was standing behind Mac. He had come back. There were a couple of people standing behind him. I called it and showed my hand—the treys. He said, 'Take it.'

"And he sat there for a long time. He didn't take another hand. He just sat there. No one said a word. And then he turned around and said, 'Okay, I'm going to play some more, so you guys have got to move.' He made everybody behind him move because he thought somebody behind him set him up. To this day, I think he thinks he got set up."

THE RAKE

Mac Fisher was set up all right—set up by himself and his betting pattern. Hoff noted that Fisher had raised every time on his deal, apparently whether he had a hand or not. Fisher was playing position the way the best players often do. When you're on the but-ton—or when you're actually dealing the cards yourself in a home game—you have the leverage of seeing everyone act first once the flop comes. You can see who's acting strong, who appears weak, what kind of hands you might be up against, and figure out how a raise might thin the field. Playing position strongly remains one of the greatest assets a player has, often greater than having a legitimate hand.

But when Fisher only called pre-flop, Hoff read weakness in his hand. Fisher's subsequent betting pattern confirmed Hoff's hunch. Fisher's bet on the Q-4-3 flop was a move to eliminate as much of the field as possible, especially the drawing hands. Fisher's bet on the flop also indicated he wasn't holding one of those cards—or even one of the small pairs—because he didn't raise pre-flop.

Understand, however, that Fisher still might have been holding one of the overcards that would have beaten Hoff and simply decided to change his pattern, calling on the button when his pattern had been to raise, to throw off his opponents. Successful players recognize they need to change their table image to keep other players guessing about the strength or weakness of their hand, but first, successful players must identify their table image.

Fisher's overbets when a queen hit the turn and a jack hit the river reeked of someone trying to buy a pot. His play didn't make sense for someone with a real hand, only someone trying to bluff. Hoff knew that if the queens or the jack had helped Fisher's hand, Fisher would have bet just enough to get a call or tried for a check-raise to maximize his hand.

♠♦ CHIP JETT ♥♣

THE BEST WAY TO EXPLAIN THE POKER SKILLS AND COMPETITIVENESS

of Chip Jett is to tell the story of the woman he won in a poker game. And the best person to tell that story is, of course, the woman herself.

"I met him in 2001 in Tunica, Mississippi, at the Jack Binion World Poker Open," the raven-haired Karina Jett begins. "I was following the tour then, but only playing side games because I didn't really know much about tournaments then and side-game action was really good.

"What happened was, I was going to Europe to play on the TV show *Late Night Poker*, and I was really nervous because I wasn't really comfortable with playing No Limit at the time. There was another poker player there, and I said, 'Why don't you all come back to my room and we'll play a satellite to help me with my No Limit game.'

"So we played, and it was kind of funny because the other guy was kind of interested in me, too, so it was like the guys were fighting for the girl with poker cards in a three-person satellite. For seven dollars. Chip only had seven dollars in his wallet. It kind of felt like whoever wins, wins the girl. And Chip won. We ended up hanging out until I went to Europe.

"Then he came out to Las Vegas for the World Series and we got married after a month and a half. We went to the drive-through chapel where Michael Jordan got married and we got married with an Elvis impersonator there."

A couple of years later, Mr. and Mrs. Poker became Mom and Pop Poker when Athena was born in October 2003. Then again, whether he's at the table or away from it, Chip Jett has always moved fast. Upon graduating from high school, he took a job as a lifeguard in his native Arizona, but then a casino opened in the area and Jett had a different idea.

"I found out how much the dealers were making—probably five or six times what lifeguards were," Jett explains. "Looked a little easier, too. So I became a dealer. Within a year, I was mostly playing. It gradually progressed to playing the biggest tournaments I could find."

Jett found so many tournaments and won so much that he says he eventually bought a home with cash by the time he was twenty. Not exactly a smart financial move, but he says he needed to show his family that he had a job and wasn't on some kind of adolescent joyride.

Upon turning twenty-one in 1995, Jett hit Las Vegas. And Las Vegas hit back, taking half of his bankroll at the blackjack tables. That's when he vowed to stick with poker.

It has worked out. In 2001, Jett was named the best all-around player at the L.A. Poker Classic. Two years later, he was named Champion of the Year—and what a year it was. He won the California State No Limit Hold'em Championship, the World Poker Open No Limit Hold'em Championship, and the L.A. Poker Classic H.O.E. title. He also placed second in the World Poker Tour Party Poker Million II main event and fourth in the WPT Legends of Poker championship.

In those years, Jett was a tournament monster, playing about 300 events a year. Since Athena's birth, he has cut that in half. "When I was chasing the [*Card Player* magazine] points title in 2003, that was too many," says Jett, who still looks as fit as a lifeguard. "At the end of the year, I was just done. I had nothing left to give. Now I wouldn't even try to do that. It kind of made me dislike poker. When it becomes a job you don't like, you should cut back because your results are going to suffer if you hate coming in to play. It should hurt to be knocked out. You shouldn't be happy about it."

But let's not kid anybody: Playing 150 tournaments a year is still a lot, because if you are good enough to play into the money, you might be playing twelve hours a day for a week.

> **H.O.E.:** An acronym for a tournament of rotating games—Hold'em, Omaha-8-or-Better, and Seven Card Stud High-Low—that change at prescribed times. (The "E" stands for "eight or better.")

Being married to a poker player also helps alleviate potential emotional pressures caused by the wild money swings inherent in the job. "There's no way that someone who doesn't play poker could ever be as understanding of certain things, like the feast-or-famine part of tournaments," Jett says. "Some months, we have a surplus of cash that's sickening. People's jaws would drop. But then there are some months where we're scraping."

To help ease their dependence on poker winnings, Chip and Karina created "Poker's Most Wanted"—a deck of playing cards that features fifty-four of the world's most renowned poker players. Fittingly, it was against one such poker player—Kenna James—that Jett pulled off a move that he cites as the best hand he ever played.

"It was in the California State Poker Championship in 2003. We were down to seven or eight players. Kenna James and I were the chip leaders. I had maybe $170,000. He had maybe $140,000.

"The blinds were probably $2,000-$4,000. A guy goes all in for $19,000. I'm the small blind, Kenna is the big blind. I ask for a countdown of his chips. I go into thought and kind of shoot Kenna a glance as if to say, 'If I call this, please don't raise.' Just a quick glance. I would never try this on anybody who's not a great, great player who wouldn't know what I was saying.

"I had two kings, and I was hoping what would happen is that when I shot him that glance, if he wakes up with anything he's going to try to take advantage of my weakness. He found two jacks."

Jett called the all in. James took the bait, raising about $80,000. When the action moved back around to Jett, he, too, moved all in.

"He's forced to call," Jett says, "even though by now he's kind of figured out what had happened. But it was too late. He had so much of his stack in there already. He decided I had A-K, or at least that's what he decided in his own mind so he could call.

"The board came blanks—no jacks—and I win a big pot and went on to win the tournament. That's the key hand that I'll always remember. Every day when you play a tournament, you have little side plans that maybe work only one in a thousand times setting people up for the future, and this was the one time the plan came together perfectly and everyone did exactly what I hoped. It's like the perfect storm."

THE RAKE

Don't try this at home. And don't take everything you see at a table at face value. It's a bit of an unwritten rule that when you get down to the end of a tournament, if a short-stacked player has called the all in, everybody else gets out of the way. The way experienced poker players convey their intentions is with the look that Jett described.

The brilliance here is that Jett acted like he was going after the small stack when he was really making a play for the big stack owned by one of the best players in any game. It involved misdirection, deceit, deception—you know, all of poker's major food groups.

Jett studied the game and broke down a millisecond of a move that happens many times in poker, and found a way to make a play with it. The difference is, Jett's move was something that could only work on a great player who was acutely attuned to the ways of poker. An inexperienced player never would have caught it.

But the lesson for the inexperienced player is to have a plan. Study the game. Pick apart your opponents and the routine of the game to find an edge.

♠◆ MEL JUDAH ♥♣

BEFORE HE MADE HIS NAME IN THE BEST POKER SALONS OF THE WORLD, Mel Judah had already found considerable fame in a very different type of salon: the kind where they cut hair. "They've overdone it on TV," the neatly coiffed, gray-haired Judah says of his previous occupation. But there's no denying that Judah was, well, a cut above the rest.

Born in India, Judah took up his mother's trade after moving to England, reaching high-profile levels while working for Vidal Sassoon, *Vogue*, and Christian Dior. He styled stars such as Goldie Hawn and Mia Farrow in the 1970s before opening a place of his own.

There is more to Judah, however, than his dexterity with scissors. After moving his family to Australia in the 1980s, he walked away from the beauty game and opened an import-export business. But that left him unsatisfied. With no interest in returning to hairdressing, Judah turned to poker after being exposed to it at the venerable Victoria Club while working in London.

"I came to poker in 1985 to have a look," he says. "I came back in 1987 to play, and then I started playing gradually, and in 1989 I won my first World Series. I decided poker was the way to go at the time because most people didn't know a lot in those days. It was pretty easy to win the money. But now it's very, very difficult."

Still, Judah has excelled. After winning his first World Series of Poker bracelet in 1989 in Seven Card Stud, he won another in the same event in 1997 while also finishing third in the WSOP main event that year. In all, he has cashed more than thirty times at the WSOP.

Judah won the World Poker Tour's Legends of Poker championship in 2003, and later that year came in sixth in the WPT's Five Diamond World Poker Classic at the Bellagio. But it was during a Pot Limit Omaha cash game in Australia that Judah found the best hand he ever played.

"The blinds were $25-$50. I'm on the big blind and I've got 2-2-3-5. The first guy raised it to $200. The next guy called $200. The next guy raised it to $600. And I called for the balance."

The flop came 2-2-5, meaning Judah flopped quad 2's. The player who raised to make it $600 had 6's and 7's. All four players checked.

"I'm going to give them free cards because I want them to have high pairs to make their full houses," Judah says. "Let them catch up." The turn came a 6. The player who had raised $600 pre-flop held 6's full of 2's.

"He decides to also check the hand down," Judah says. "I don't know what he's thinking. It's wrong for him to do that, but he did.

"The river card comes a 10. Now another guy has 2's full of 10's. I bet on the river about $2,000. The pot was $2,400. I got raised the pot The other guy called. Then I moved in, and the other guys went call, call. There was about $28,000 in the pot at the end."

THE RAKE

When you flop a monster hand such as quads or something close to the stone nuts, you have to figure out how to extract as much money as possible, and that usually involves checking and calling before making your big bet or raising on the river. There are two reasons for that: You have to allow your opponents to build hands they can bet with, and also you are showing some weakness by not raising, thus making opponents more confident in betting when they think they have drawn out to the best hand.

As long as Judah held the nuts with his quad deuces, he was willing to take cards off, knowing he could not make much money betting out or raising on the flop or the turn. This is especially true in any kind of Pot Limit game, because the biggest bet can match only the amount in the pot, as compared to the way you can move all in at any time in a No Limit game.

Conventional strategy in Pot Limit compels you to bet out when holding a set or a middle full house. That's why Judah couldn't understand why his opponent holding 6's full of 2's had checked the hand down.

Cashed: To have finished in a payout spot in a tournament. **Raised the pot:** The maximum raise in a Pot Limit game. **Middle full house:** When your set in a full house is comprised of 6's, 7's, 8's or 9's.

The funny thing is, that particular opponent adopted Judah's strategy of checking and calling because he, too, was letting opponents catch up so he could bet out big on the river. He just didn't realize he was so far behind Judah.

♠♦ THOMAS KELLER ♥♣

THE STORY GOES THAT THOMAS KELLER HAD AN ARIZONA CASINO'S INVENTORY of black chips in the trunk of his car. Rack after rack after rack. Said to be worth more than a million bucks. Right there in his car.

Then one day the big-money cash game players wanted to play a big-money cash game, but there were no black $100 chips anywhere inside the building. And so, the story concludes, Keller went to his car and started selling off racks worth $10,000 a pop.

Great story. And the best part is, some of it is even true.

"I did have a lot of the black chips," Keller explains with a laugh, "but they weren't in my car. I had a locker at the club. It was just easier, when I left a game, to keep the chips and use them next time instead of cashing in each time."

This story of how Keller emptied the stash in his locker does a wonderful job of explaining how he dominated his local high-stakes cash games, which helped him become the kind of championship player he is today.

An outsized character with round features and a bubbling personality—think John Candy with Big Slick—the Michigan native came to poker after earning an economics degree from Stanford. He began playing serious tournament poker in 2003, winning the $2,500 buy-in No Limit Hold'em event at the Bellagio and finishing third in a Limit Hold'em event at the Commerce Casino.

Keller and his fiancée, Andra, got married in April 2004, but agreed to a shortened honeymoon so he could compete in his first World Series of Poker No Limit Hold'em championship. But first, Keller entered the $5,000 buy-in No Limit Hold'em event "so I wouldn't be rusty."

Some rust. Keller busted **Martin de Knijff** with a full house over a full house in heads-up play, and collected more than $382,000 and his first bracelet in the first World Series of Poker event he had ever played. At twenty-three, he became one of the youngest bracelet winners of all time.

And yet, Keller says the best hand he ever played was the one that knocked him out of the $10,000 buy-in No Limit Hold'em championship at the 2004 L.A. Poker Classic at the Commerce Casino.

"I had been playing very aggressively for several hours and had built a large stack, $75,000 in chips, which was in the top five with about 100 players left. The blinds were $500-$1,000, with $100 antes. The action started off quiet enough, with everyone folding to the small blind, who completed his blind, and then the action came to me in the big blind. I looked down to see a rag, Q-8 offsuit, a hand with which I would normally check in this spot and see a flop. However, I thought the small blind was very weak by the way he painfully threw his chips in to complete his blind, so I raised the pot $2,000, figuring he would fold and I would pick up the blinds and antes right then and there."

Much to Keller's surprise, the small blind re-raised him $7,500. Most players in Keller's position would fold because it looked like the small blind was trying to trap him with a big hand.

"I still had a lot of faith in my initial read that my opponent was weak," Keller says. "There were many other factors involved, as well. I had been playing very aggressively, and was sure that my opponent knew this and could definitely be on a re-steal with a marginal hand, figuring, quite correctly, that I was just trying to steal the pot with my initial raise. He also had a large stack, so I was getting substantial implied odds if I could bust him on this hand. I quickly concluded that he either had a huge hand with which he was going to commit all of his chips, or a marginal hand and was just trying to re-steal.

"I considered re-raising him, but figured I would need to re-raise at least another $15,000 to make the raise look legitimate and get him to fold a marginal hand. I also was worried that he would still think I was on a steal and would try to re-steal again with an all-in move or another big raise on top of whatever I raised. I did not want to put $22,500 into the pot pre-flop and have to fold if he then moved all in on me. At the same time, I did not want to fold. Given all of these factors, I decided to just call his raise with the intention of making a move on him post-flop, unless I actually flopped a hand."

Keller called. The flop came K-3-2 with two spades. The small blind led into the $22,000 pot with only a $6,000 bet.

"I thought this was a very weak bet and contemplated raising him to try to pick up the $28,000 pot," Keller says. "However, I really believed that just calling might actually look stronger, as it often does in No Limit Hold'em, since raising or betting with nothing is a standard play because you are putting pressure on your opponent to fold." Keller called with his queen-high.

The turn came a 10, and the small blind checked. "I bet $10,000 into the $34,000 pot," Keller says. "Now that was a smallish bet for that pot, but it was a reasonable bet given his

Flopped a hand: To develop a good holding after the first three community cards are exposed.

chip stack, as the bet was more than 10 percent of his total stack and I figured he would fold a nothing hand to that bet, especially given the way I had played the hand. I also figured that if he just called that smallish bet he was not that strong, and if a blank came off on the end I could move in and he likely would not be able to call."

The small blind called. The river came a 6 of spades, making a flush possible. "My opponent checked immediately," Keller says, "and I quickly moved all in for my remaining $40,000. I never put him on a flush draw, given how he had played the hand, and I thought the 6 was about as harmless a card as could come. He went into deep thought for what seemed like several minutes. I'm getting nervous. My entire tournament rested on this hand, and I knew there was no way I could be good if he called. Finally, he said those dreaded words: 'I call.'

"I knew my hand was beat, but I had to see what he had called me with, so I flipped over my measly Q-8. He immediately flipped over a total rag, 10-6 offsuit, giving him runner-runner two pair. The entire table was shocked by the weak hands that were turned over in the biggest pot of the tournament up to that point. As the dealer pushed my opponent the $140,000 pot, my mind raced with thoughts of how I could have played the hand differently. I was happy that at least my read was right, that he was making a re-steal, because in the long run this hand would give me crucial confidence to trust future reads and follow my instincts. I obviously wish I had won the pot, but I am satisfied with how I played the hand.

"And remember one thing: If you're going to bluff off your big stack in one hand in a huge tournament, make sure you at least get a good story out of it."

THE RAKE

Thomas Keller made the right read on the kind of hand he believed his opponent was holding. And he made the right moves based on that read. And then the deck came badly for him and he was out of the tournament after amassing one of the biggest stacks at the time. Such are the vagaries of poker.

But Keller's play provides a wonderful guide to the kind of thinking that goes into a bluff, especially when it involves two big stacks.

First, Keller's decision to raise the small blind with Q-8 in the big blind is a pretty standard play in trying to steal the blinds and antes. His opponent's re-raise gave him reason for concern, and he called only because he would have position the rest of the hand. This is not a play you can make against a big stack when you are out of position.

Note how Keller's pre-flop thinking included two moves on the flop: one if he missed it, one if he hit it. And he planned his betting down to the river. The key to a successful bluff is to make sure the betting pattern makes sense—that you bet the hand the way you would if you actually held what you were representing.

When Keller's opponent made a weak bet on the flop that missed both players, Keller chose to call, figuring he was showing strength, and here's why: Calling a bet when the pot is already big generally means that you must have some sort of hand if you are not going to try to win the pot right there. It looks like you are trying to string along your opponent and allows you to take down the pot on the turn with any kind of bet. The danger, of course, is that you give your opponent another card that could help his hand, which is what happened when the 10 on the turn paired up Keller's opponent.

Keller made a $10,000 bet into a $34,000 pot that he believed was big enough to cause his opponent to fold, and it should have been if his opponent believed Keller was holding the type of hand he was representing. Keller's bet gave his opponent 3.4-1 odds, which can be enticing, but if Keller was holding a king, his opponent was almost a 9-1 underdog with one card to come.

In hindsight, any kind of raise of his opponent's weak bet on the K-2-3 flop probably would've convinced his opponent to muck his 10-6 offsuit in the face of a likely pair of kings.

The irony is, Keller still probably would have won the hand if anything other than a 6 or a 10 came on the river. The 6, in fact, is the only card that could break Keller. It's highly unlikely that his opponent would call Keller's all in with just a pair of 10's, and if a 10 had come on the end, his opponent would have bet out, or if he had checked a set of 10's, Keller would not have risked all his chips with the board paired, fearing a trap. Walking out of the tournament stunned, Keller took from the hand the confidence to trust his read. He viewed that as crucial, and you have to believe him, seeing as how he won the $5,000 buy-in No Limit Hold'em tournament at the World Series of Poker a couple of months later.

♠ ◆ PHIL LAAK ♥ ♣

YOU DON'T TALK TO PHIL LAAK AS MUCH YOU EXPERIENCE HIM. Easily animated and given to a hyper speech pattern, the Dublin-born Laak might be the most entertaining poker player going, whether he's bouncing around the table as the cards are dealt, kneeling beside the dealer in an effort to bring good flops, or thrashing all over the floor upon hitting a miracle card.

His act, of course, starts with his trademark gray hooded sweatshirt and sunglasses, earning him the eminently marketable moniker The Unabomber.

"Some guy in New York gave me the nickname," Laak explains. "I was always wearing it. It was a function thing to start. The poker club was a little bit drafty and it was cold on the way to getting there. The shades for the hangover—it was beautiful. Then I realized it was genius. I could shield myself from all the people that could read me."

Before learning poker in 1999, Laak lived many lives: He was a repo man, ran sports bets, managed a hedge fund, studied mechanical engineering, tried day trading, was a backgammon junkie, and hoped to be a wizard software programmer. All before the age of thirty. "I was using my brains to crowbar money out of the universe," he says.

Laak blew into America's living rooms during the second season of the World Poker Tour when he won the WPT Invitational at the Commerce Casino, finished fourth in the Bad Boys of Poker event at the Bellagio, and took sixth in the Legends of Poker at the Bicycle Club.

The Unabomber says the best hand he ever played came early in his career, against good friend and former roommate **Antonio Esfandiari.**

"We're in the Commerce Casino. I'd been playing cards for, I don't know, less than two years, more than six months. It's no-limit, cash game. There are some twisted things about this hand. One, I had bought into the game for, like, $10,000 and drifted down to like $5,000. Antonio had everyone covered in spades.

"Antonio had just made a disparaging remark about how tight I was playing: 'What are you afraid of? Why, don't you have me covered?'

"I said, 'You want me to go to the box? I'll go to the box right now.'

"He goes, 'Yeah, yeah, yeah.'

"We both had boxes for cash at the Commerce. He wanted me to reload. If somebody challenges me, I love it. I just needed a little motivation to go to the box. There are times where I haven't gone to the box because I didn't want to miss a hand. This was playing normal, so I timed it with a bathroom break and a big hand to minimize the number of hands I lost.

"I come back and load up. I have around $5,000 more. I was in seat two and Antonio was in seat seven or eight. Antonio had two 7's. I had Q-Q. The flop came 6-7-2, with two hearts. One guy had a flush draw, one guy had a straight draw, Antonio had top set, and I had an overpair.

"On the flop, there was some skirmishing. It was really weird. I knew everyone had a hand, and I was the last one to act. Antonio checked. I made a small bet. Call. Call. Antonio raised, and I raised again about another $1,000."

The turn came a queen, giving Laak top set, and Esfandiari checked. Laak bet about $500 and Esfandiari raised $1,000. Laak re-raised $4,500.

Box: Many poker rooms have something akin to safe-deposit boxes where players can store chips so they don't have to go through the cash exchange buy-in routine.

"Antonio had a tough spot. He can't call. He has to fold or go all in. If he calls, if I'm on a draw, he gives me a free way to get there. He thinks forever, and I think, oh, my god, he has a set. There's only one hand that's beating him, which is two queens. I'm like, could he put me on that hand?"

Apparently not, because Esfandiari moved in for the roughly $7,000 that Laak had in front of him, and Laak called. The river came an 8. No help to anyone. Laak wins.

"He was so sick. He almost folded. Later he was telling me he was around 40 percent to fold. I scooped the biggest pot I had ever won at that time—strange money; money that's not yours. It was about $15,000 from Antonio and $3,000 or $4,000 from the other guys. The pot was $30,000-something. It was so sick."

THE RAKE

Reading people and their hands after the flop might be the most expensive or profitable thing you ever do in No Limit Hold'em. It requires far greater poker savvy than simply going all in before the flop. It requires thinking ahead to the river. If your opponent might be bluffing and you have a real hand, it's often wise to keep your action to a minimum and hope your opponent hangs himself on the river. Let him bet your hand in an attempt to buy it. But if you know your opponent has a hand he loves—if you really feel it—and you also have a hand you love and you know you're going to call him on the river anyway, you should go all in right there. If you have the best hand at that point, you have a chance to win more. If you're behind, you put pressure on your opponent with your aggressive play and perhaps win the pot right there if your opponent folds. If your opponent is bluffing while trying to hit a draw, you are making him pay for it.

♠♦ HOWARD LEDERER ♥♣

LIFE WAS ALWAYS FUN AND GAMES FOR HOWARD LEDERER. WELL IT WAS ALWAYS games. "I was accepted at Columbia," Lederer says, explaining how he discovered poker in the early 1980s. "I deferred for a year, started playing chess. That summer, I found the poker game in the back room of the chess hall. I literally ended up moving into the chess hall—working, running errands for the club, playing cheap poker, going broke over and over again, doing whatever. I was eighteen—didn't care.

Lederer, whose imposing 6'5" frame is at least as intimidating as his weapons-grade stare and computer-like mind, did not start winning at poker for a couple of years, just as he began taking classes at Columbia. "I had this year where I made $100,000 in poker, which was just incredible money to me back then," he says, "and I did it by going to school at eight in the morning, doing my coursework 'til three, heading down to the poker game, starting at four, playing until at least midnight, getting some homework done, getting to bed at three, waking up at seven, and doing it all over again. At the end of that year, I was just toast. Absolute toast. And I knew I had to make a decision."

Actually, the decision seemed to be made the year before by an unlikely source: his professorial father, who was then an instructor at a New Hampshire prep school and the author of *Anguished English*—and would appear to be the last person to approve of a son mucking an Ivy League education for poker.

But Richard Lederer cut an independent swath of his own. He was the first member of his family not to enter the family ribbon business in Philadelphia. Accepted at Harvard Law School, Lederer *père* simply decided he would rather devote himself to teaching.

"He never lost that sense that he had gone his own way," Howard Lederer says of his father. "I remember very distinctly being in New York, playing cheap poker, not doing well, not going to college—and he's a dad, he's concerned. He came to New York, visited with me, but he also sat down with the guy who was running the poker game and said, 'Does Howard have some potential? Do you think he could be a good poker player?' And the guy told him he thought I could. My dad said, 'Okay, I'll give him another year.' He wanted to make sure I wasn't completely tossing my life out the window. By the end of that second year, I started doing well."

And he shows no signs of slowing down. The forty-two-year-old Lederer has already won two World Series of Poker bracelets and captured two titles in the World Poker Tour's first season.

He was, of course, also instrumental in making professional poker a family affair, encouraging his sister **Annie Duke** to take up the game. She not only has gone on a remarkable run of her own, but she has occasionally knocked out her big brother in big tournaments, including the $2 million winner-take-all World Series of Poker Tournament of Champions in 2004.

The schooling that Lederer gives opponents at the tables has also earned him the nickname The Professor of Poker, thanks to player/broadcaster Jesse May. "I was doing commentary with him and that name just stuck," Lederer says. "I think there's some validity to it in terms of my approach to the game, so I'm not objecting to it. I have had people walk up to me and say, 'You're a professor of what?' "

Lederer says the best hand he ever played—or, perhaps more precisely, "my most important" hand—came in 1987 during his first World Series of Poker, when he made the final table of the world championship event.

"I had tried to get into the tournament through one-table satellites—they didn't have supersatellites back then—in 1986, and I'd failed. I'd given myself a three-satellite budget, $3,000, to get in and I failed, so I was excited to be playing in my first final event of the World Series.

"I think it was 163 players, and I'd had a very fortunate run and I was at the final table. We're down to five players, and **Johnny Chan** has most of the chips at the table. He's dominating the table, and he's the best player."

Lederer had about $60,000, Chan more than $300,000. With the blinds at $1,500-$3,000, Lederer drew pocket 3's one off the button. He made it $9,000 to go. In the big blind, Chan called and the flop came J-9-4.

"Not a very good flop for a pair of 3's. Johnny checks, and I check. He's a rather intimidating guy, so I'm just kind of waiting to see what happens. Obviously, I'm hoping for a 3. The next card comes up, and it's a deuce.

"Now also, this is the first time I've played poker in front of an audience. There's probably a good audience of a hundred there watching, and it's pretty intense, at least for me. I was twenty-three at the time.

"There's a little over $20,000 in the pot and he bets about $15,000. And it hits me that my 3's are good. He's got all the chips at the table, he's going to be trying to run me over, but I'm just pretty sure I have the best hand. I don't know what it was. I was almost certain I had the best hand. It was one of those things—a physical tell, a situational tell, it was a lot of those things, and it just all came together.

"But I'm in a position where, if I have the best hand and I raise all in, the hand's over and I win his $15,000, plus the pot. But if I'm wrong—and certainly I could be wrong—I'm going to lose all my chips. So if I'm going to play this hand, if I'm going to try to find out if I have the right hand, I kind of need to be willing to risk all my chips.

"If I'm really convinced he's bluffing, then maybe I let him bluff some more. So at least I have a chance to win as many chips as I'm risking. Because if I raise all in, I'm risking all my chips, but I can only win the $15,000, plus the pot. Also, I want to encourage him as best as possible to bluff on the river. Kind of importantly, the deuce that came up put two diamonds out there.

"Anyway, I decide that I'm going to do everything I can to convince Johnny Chan that I have a draw. I count down the pot, I count out the chips that I have to call, I count out how much I have left. I really make it look like I'm calculating. I really did trot out a little Hollywood. I just wanted to convince him that I'd have to be drawing. So I went through my little act and I called. I called as meekly and as scared as I could.

"The last card was actually the best card in the deck—a 4, so the board paired 4's. Another 3 would be the best, obviously, but if I had the best hand on the turn, I still had the best hand here."

At that point, Lederer had about $42,000 left, and the pot contained about $50,000. Chan bet Lederer all in.

"My chips beat him into the pot. Once I made that commitment on fourth street, there was no looking back. If he was going to bet, I was going to call him, so I didn't waste any time. I just called him instantly. And he rapped the table and I won. Didn't flip over his cards.

"It's the most important because it showed me for the first time that I can actually outplay a great player. Maybe not all day yet, but at least for a hand. It gave me confidence.

"I finished fifth in that tournament, so winning that hand didn't win me any money. I was the next guy out. I haven't really talked about that hand to a lot of people, but that's the hand that I could think about when I needed confidence, when I needed to convince myself that I belonged in a game or that I had the potential to be a great player. I was able to draw on that hand for mental strength. I think everyone needs that."

THE RAKE

Every great—or even good—poker player has a hand where he starts believing in himself, starts believing he can play with, and perhaps outplay, those with more talent, and this was Howard Lederer's.

If you had to pinpoint the moment it began, it would be fourth street. Lederer checked on the flop because Chan had established himself as the best player, and you could count his chips if you needed any explanation. Lederer wanted to see what Chan would do, which was to check behind Lederer.

But the epiphany came on fourth street. Holding a pair of 3's, Lederer watched a deuce turn, making the board J-9-4-2. Not much help to pocket 3's. But when Chan bet $15,000 into a $20,000 pot, he was trying to indicate strength. Lederer, however, read it as weakness—an overbet that represented the strength of Chan's chips and table image, but not his hand. There is, of course, a big difference, and it struck Lederer at the right time. That is when Lederer determined that Chan was trying to run him off his hand.

Now take note of the way that the World Series of Poker rookie did not make the rookie mistake of going all in when Chan led out $15,000. Lederer knew that if he moved in, he could win the pot and only the additional $15,000 that Chan bet, but he would be risking his entire stack, about triple Chan's bet. So Lederer found a way to get Chan to commit just as many chips by working some Actor's Studio into his game, pretending he was on a draw and afraid of Chan's holdings.

And Chan bought it. When the river paired 4's, Chan continued trying to buy the pot by moving Lederer all in, which was exactly what Lederer wanted and was prepared for. Notice how Lederer played fifth street at the same time he planned his strategy on fourth. It cannot be stressed enough how you have to spin every possible option on each street.

Obviously, Lederer was hoping for a 3 to hit the board and make a set, which would have let him exhale a little bit. But let's look at the problem of playing small pairs: Even when you flop a set, you are almost always worried about facing a bigger set, but you cannot live in fear of set over set, particularly in tournaments.

♠ ◆ KATHY LIEBERT ♥ ♣

KATHY LIEBERT JUST WASN'T INTO THE NINE-TO-FIVE LIFE. WHICH CAN BE QUITE A problem for someone with a business degree from Marist College and a job as a business analyst at the prestigious Dun & Bradstreet. Even worse for someone considering law school.

So Liebert eventually settled in Colorado and called her own hours, playing poker at night and cagily making investments during the stock boom of the 1990s that earned her financial independence.

Playing more tournaments, Liebert eventually moved to Las Vegas and got noticed. In 1997 and 1998, she made the top twelve in the *Card Player* Tournament Player of the Year rankings. In 2000, she was the chip leader after day two of the World Series of Poker championship and was being touted by many as the best female poker player going.

Liebert broke through a couple of years later when she walked off with major titles in two different series. In 2002, she boarded a ship and came home with the World Poker Tour's Party Poker Million title and the $1 million top prize. But validation for almost every poker player comes at the World Series of Poker and gaining that precious bracelet. In 2004, she captured the $1,500 buy-in Limit Hold'em Shootout event. As you might expect, Liebert says the best hand she ever played came during her bracelet-winning event.

"I was heads up with Kevin Song," Liebert says. "I had a 4-3 suited. I came in, he re-raised, I called." The flop came small cards with three clubs. Liebert flopped bottom pair. Song bet and Liebert raised. Another small card came on the turn.

"What was memorable about it was that on the river, a fourth club came on the board. He bet out and I called him with bottom pair. There are four clubs out there, four overcards out there, but I didn't believe it based on the sequence of his actions.

"The pot was big enough to risk it. People were in shock that I called on the river. He was a little more intimidated because I called the bluff. He was kind of like, 'Whoa, how could you call with that hand?' I wound up winning that tournament."

THE RAKE

It seems like such a simple little hand. But so many things happened here to turn the event into a bracelet for Kathy Liebert. First, there was Liebert's decision to play a couple of small cards—yet another example of how any two cards can win. In those situations where you find yourself playing a greater range of hands, it is more important how you bet and how you read your opponent's betting pattern than what you hold.

If a player raises before the flop, he is probably holding big cards. This is far more likely in limit because limit is a big-card game. But if the board comes small, even if it is suited, and the pre-flop raiser does not play it strong, he is probably hoping to get a free card that pairs him up.

In this case, Kevin Song re-raised Liebert pre-flop, which showed strength. But when Song didn't re-raise Liebert after the flop—and then checked on the turn when another small card came—Liebert stuck with her read that he was playing big cards and looking to draw out to a pair.

Draw out: To have the remaining board cards make your hand.

Song bet out on the river when a fourth club fell, so the risk for Liebert was she would have been trapped if Song had been slow-playing big flush cards. But the size of the pot and her read prompted her to call him down.

Liebert's gutsy play points out how one pot can change an opponent's game by changing his mindset. Calling someone's bluff with a small hand and winning the pot—especially in the face of so many overcards and big hands that were possible given that board—can intimidate a player.

Liebert believes that hand intimidated Song as the tournament wore on, and made him reluctant to take big shots at a pot. He became more predictable in subsequent hands he would play, giving Liebert not only the ability to narrow the range of hands she was up against, but also enabling her to play aggressively with lesser hands because Song was cautious about risking his stack.

The bottom line is, any time you can put your opponent on a hand and your opponent is afraid of what you are playing, you are golden.

♠ ♦ ERICK LINDGREN ♥ ♣

ERICK LINDGREN WILL BET ON SPORTING EVENTS, WAGER ON THE GOLF COURSE AND shoot free throws for money in his Las Vegas backyard with fellow star poker players Phil Ivey and **Gus Hansen**. "The only thing I don't gamble on is poker," Lindgren quips. "When it's poker, I try to take the best of it."

It is that businesslike attitude that has made the twenty-nine-year-old Lindgren one of the most feared young players in the game today. E-dog, as he is known to friends, earned the World Poker Tour's inaugural Player of the Year award in 2004, which included winning the Party Poker Million III. Coming into 2004, Lindgren had won the Ultimate Poker Classic in 2003 and the Five Diamond World Poker Classic in 2002.

Lindgren, who was an all-league high school quarterback in football and was league MVP in basketball in his small California town of Burney, came to poker after his athletic career ended in college. "They tried to make me into a point guard, but I was much more of a shooter," he recalls. "Growing up on the dirt court, it just didn't work. My handle was an embarrassment, and it still is. But I can shoot the rock."

At the same time, Lindgren and some of his friends found an Indian casino that allowed outsiders to pay $5 for a six-deck blackjack shoe and act as the house by dealing. But Lindgren's blackjack dealing days ended when he discovered the poker room in the back and started winning.

"I was playing small limits at the time—$3-$6, $6-$12—but I was supporting myself," he says. "Then I gradually moved up and played bigger." Nowadays, Lindgren, who spends about ten hours a week online at fulltiltpoker.com, plays in the biggest tournaments around, such as the Ultimate Poker Classic, where in 2003 he says the best hand he ever played took place.

"It was heads-up and I was up against Daniel Larson. I had worn the guy down from about $3.6 million to about $600,000. I've got a pretty big lead. He called on the button. I don't know if it meant he has a big hand. It could have been a big hand, it could have been aces, or it could have meant he just wanted to see the flop."

The blinds were $80,000-$160,000, which benefited a big stack such as Lindgren's. But there was a twist: The World Poker Tour did not have a lot of videotape remaining, so the blind intervals were increasing faster than usual. That, in turn, forced Lindgren and Larson to play a wider range of hands more aggressively.

"I was dealt the Q-3 of diamonds in the big blind. I figured it was better than a 50-50 hand. He could've limped with a 7-high, 8-high, something that he may not be able to call with. There was so much money in there that I felt if there was any chance of him folding, I needed to push in. So that's what I did. He had to call about $400,000 more.

"He immediately called me, and I said uh oh. I thought I had walked into aces. But he just had A-K. It's not that bad of a situation. I'm about a 2-1 dog. The flop came a queen and the turn a 3, and I secured my first television victory and half a million dollars. It was my first major win, my first televised tournament win. You don't know how often you're going to get there at that point. It's so key to get that.

"You get there, and second would be a disaster. There was a lot of pressure on me because when we got heads-up, I had a big chip lead, so to blow that would've been absolutely brutal. It was more relief than anything that I didn't blow it."

THE RAKE

A-K, of course, is one of the best starting hands in Hold'em, but the decision is how big you want to play it. Larson wanted to play it big enough to double up by trying to trap Lindgren. That's why he called on the button instead of going all in pre-flop.

Had Larson moved in pre-flop, he likely would have taken the blinds and the antes and moved on to the next hand because Lindgren felt the pressure of having a big chip lead.

A major factor in the hand was the quickly increasing blind structure. Here's what that does: It forces you to play a wider variety of hands and to play them more aggressively, but it also means that you will see fewer hands, which means you will see fewer great starting hands, so you make a decision how to get the most out of them.

Shorter blind intervals help the less experienced player because the pros prefer to see a lot of flops as a way of gaining information. That enables pros to run more bluffs, to draw chips from an opponent as a way of getting him committed to the pot, and to identify when an opponent is trying to pull off a bluff himself.

So you can see why Larson just chose to call the blind. He did not know when he would see such a good starting hand again and felt the best way to maximize his A-K in his uphill battle was to make Lindgren think he was weak. That he lost the hand is probably more of a credit to Lindgren's poker instincts.

♠♦ MARCEL LUSKE ♥♣

TELEVISED POKER WAS MADE FOR MARCEL LUSKE. OR PERHAPS IT IS THE OTHER WAY around. Consider the way he dresses: the dapper Dutchman usually wears a sharply cut suit at the table, which clearly puts him in *GQ*'s starting poker lineup. Then, when he dons his baseball cap and sunglasses that he often sports upside down, well, sometimes you *can* tell the players without a scorecard.

Even if you couldn't see Luske at a table, you certainly can hear him—whether he is delivering a monologue or just singing whatever tune fits the situation. But don't be fooled by the act. The man can play. And he can do it with some flat-out mystical brilliance.

"I do like to joke and play with people at the table—play with their minds, get under their skin and be active," Luske admits. "That's why a game like this in tournaments suits me better, because I have a lot of chips and I can move. I don't mind losing a few hands, but when they don't expect it, I can really hit them, and hit them hard. They can win a little, a little, a little, and then suddenly, I get my hand and they'll wonder how I can play it—and they'll never expect the move."

The Amsterdam-born Luske began playing cards when he was five years old and eventually graduated to playing poker with friends and competing in tournaments. "I started to win tournaments and I thought most people don't know what's going on at the table," Luske says. "They take chances in positions they shouldn't be in. So they're telling me, Pick up the money; it's there for you. *Somebody* has to pick it up."

A black belt in karate, the tall, strawberry blond held a day job as a real estate contract negotiator until early in 2004. "If you look at the money in poker, it's much better than to go to work at nine o'clock in the morning," the fifty-two-year-old Luske says.

Luske says the best hand he ever played came during the World Poker Tour's Five Diamond Poker Classic at the Bellagio in 2004.

"The blinds were $100-$200 and I raised it to $500 under the gun. I had jacks and the guy re-raised $1,500 behind me to eliminate the field. He had a little bit more in chips than me. So I called him $1,000 more. I still had $2,925 and I wanted to see the flop."

The flop came K-9-5, with two spades. Luske checked, and his opponent bet $2,800. "I looked at him and I looked at the flop. I considered that he re-raised me before the flop. It looks very likely that he has A-K, but as I look at the guy, I told him I'm going to raise him $125 more, and if he shows me A-K I will have a nice break and I will have a total misread.

"He paid the $125 more and I said, 'According to my imagination, you're going to show me two 10's.' And I opened my jacks and while he was opening his cards he showed two 10's and they fell out of his hands, like he was amazed. The whole table was like, how did you do that?

"It *was* quite amazing. I didn't think he had A-K there because he would play it differently. He would not make a big bet to try to get me out if he had that or aces, kings, or queens. In order to protect his hand, he would make a big bet if he had a smaller pair. The fact he raised me before the flop looked like he knew that I could re-raise him for $2,925. And he thought about this without seeing the flop. So in my imagination, he must have a made hand.

"It's easy to say these things after the hand, but I didn't say this after the hand. I did it before the hand. It proves to them that I must know something they don't know. What I try to say is that in these days when you have computers calculating things so quickly and you have an outcome within a second, we used to take a minute or two minutes to make some calculations and write them down on paper. If you're an experienced poker player, you know to analyze things, and then you know to eliminate things—like he couldn't have pocket kings or aces.

Made hand: A hand that doesn't need improvement to win. **Out of position:** When your spot in the betting rotation comes before your opponents, meaning you don't have the advantage of seeing all the action before you must make a move.

"Therefore I came to the judgment that he had two 10's because that was the exact amount he would bet at that moment if he had two 10's."

THE RAKE

Is it any wonder that Marcel Luske has an intimidating table image? And to pull off that little bit of magic with jacks, one of the most troubling hands in No Limit Hold'em, and to do it while out of position underscores his remarkable abilities.

Pocket jacks are good enough to keep you close and bad enough to get you beat. If you see a flop with jacks and want to find out how strong they really are, the answer is not very—especially if the flop comes A-K or K-Q.

When the king fell in this hand, Luske checked to see what his opponent's next move would tell him about the strength of his hand. It turns out, it told him a lot. Luske analyzed his opponent, his position at the table and his spot in that very hand, and was not only able to put him on a hand, but was able to put his opponent on *the* hand. Luske deduced that the overbet was his opponent's attempt to represent a king in his hand to match the one on the board and to run off Luske if he was trying to draw to, say, A-Q or A-J. So Luske took the bet to mean his opponent held some lesser cards.

A small bet would have encouraged Luske to take off another card, but would have left him concerned that he was facing an overpair and was being strung along, a play that might have worked if it was followed by a bigger bet on the turn. In fact, Luske says he would have been most worried about a check from his opponent on the flop because that is the way you play big pairs or a set of kings.

♠♦ MATT MATROS ♥♣

FROM A B.S. IN MATHEMATICS AT YALE TO AN M.F.A. IN FICTION WRITING AT Sarah Lawrence to big-time poker? It might not be the most obvious career path, but then, poker is all about knowing numbers and reading people (if not writing about them). At any rate, this academic route has certainly worked out for Matt Matros. In 2004, he finished third in the World Poker Tour Championship at the Bellagio, collecting $706,903 and providing a new ending to his book *The Making of a Poker Player.*

A native New Yorker, Matros began playing poker with school pals, but the high school valedictorian didn't study it seriously until he neared graduation from Yale. Three years into life as a software quality engineer, Matros quit to attend Sarah Lawrence. After his first year of graduate school, he signed a book deal and played poker all summer, doing well enough to pay for his second year of graduate school.

These days, the twenty-eight-year-old Matros is working as a writer, poker player, and coach, so if the point of college is to teach you how to make money, Matros has found a way to get to the top of his class again.

Matros says the best hand he ever played came during the second day of his spectacular run in the 2004 World Poker Tour Championship.

"Seated to my left," he explains, "was a poker rarity, a female professional. She was super-nice, engaging in conversation from the outset, and I had every indication that she was a tough, solid, experienced player. I had yet to tangle with her before the hand." With the blinds at $400-$800 and a $100 ante, Matros opened for $2,600 in late position with a J and an 8 of diamonds. "The woman to my left said, 'Raise. Make it $5,000.' It was a miniscule re-raise, but it scared the hell out of me. I figured her for kings or aces, and thought it almost impossible that she could have anything else. The blinds folded. I called for several reasons—one of the most important being that I didn't want to have people re-raising me for the rest of the day."

The flop came Q-J-7, with two more diamonds. Matros checked, intending to fold his middle pair/no kicker hand to any bet. "Except she only bet $2,000 into the $12,100 pot. So I called again, thinking I was now getting a price to draw out on K-K or A-A.

"The turn brought the ace of diamonds. I felt this was one of the best cards I could hope for. If my opponent had two kings—especially without the king of diamonds—she might well have given up the hand to a bet. Even with a set of aces, she had to be worried I had just made a flush.

"I lead out for $6,000, thinking there was a chance my opponent would fold and that it would be almost impossible for her to raise. 'Raise' was the next word out of her mouth. Damn, I thought, so much for making a play at this pot. And then something strange happened.

"My opponent tried to make it a total of $4,000. It was then she realized that I had bet $6,000—a $5,000 chip and two $500 chips. I had not, as she had originally thought, bet $1,200—a $1,000 chip and two $100 chips. But I said, 'Raise.' She said. 'I raise. I make it $12,000.'

"With some players, I would've been worried. Less-than-scrupulous folks might have done something like this as an angle with the nuts. But I had played with this woman long enough to be confident she wasn't angling. She was a stand-up person and player. I was equally confident she didn't have two diamonds in her hand. So what to do about this?

"I could have folded, of course. I was sure my opponent had a much bigger hand than I did. I could've called the $6,000, accepting the price she was offering for my 8-high flush draw. Or I could see how much she really liked her hand. Did she really want to call an all-in re-raise from me with two kings, with or without a diamond? Hell, did she really want to call with a set of aces?

"I decided she didn't, and that if god forbid she did call me, I still had some outs against her likely holdings. 'I'm all-in,' I said, raising her $25,000 more. When my opponent failed to call instantly, I knew there was a chance the play would work. This knowledge didn't make me any less petrified as I sat there, for minutes, with all my chips in the middle, as she deliberated. I didn't dare say anything. I didn't dare look at her. I try never to do those things anyway, but this was the only time in my poker career I was actually scared to do or say anything. I had never put

Late position: Generally considered the spot at the table where the button sits, and the two positions to the right of it. Price: Pot odds. Outs: The unexposed cards remaining that would make your hand. If you have no outs when there are still cards to be exposed on the board, you are said to be drawing dead. Protector: An object that players put on their cards when they play a hand. It can be anything from a stack of chips to a good-luck charm to even fossils, which is what Greg Raymer used in the 2004 World Series of Poker main event to become known as Fossilman. The function of protectors is to make sure the dealer doesn't grab your cards and shove them into the muck, thereby killing your hand. Underbet: A bet that is less than expected for the size of the pot. Sometimes it is a strategy ploy to get an opponent to call. Sometimes it is a probe bet to determine the strength of your opponent's hand.

a player on a range as strong as kings or aces and tried to move that player off the hand, and now I was doing it in the WPT Championship.

"Finally, my opponent took her protector off her cards. She waited a few more seconds, just to be sure—and then she slid her hand into the muck. I heard later, reliably, that she had thrown away pocket queens which, in case you weren't counting, gave her three of them. Re-raising all in in this spot was probably the gutsiest thing I have ever done."

THE RAKE

Think of this hand as a portrait of the artist as a young poker player. Matros made a raise pre-flop in an attempt to steal the blinds with a marginal J-8. When his opponent played back at him with a re-raise, Matros banked some credit for his hand and his table image by calling to show he wouldn't get raised out of every pot all day.

The Q-J-7 flop that gave Matros a middle pair with a weak kicker presents a great example of how you must be able to change strategy based on the board and your read on your opponent's betting. He was ready to fold, but the curious underbet by Matros' opponent gave him good odds to stick around and try to draw out.

If Matros was facing aces, he was a 4-1 underdog, but his opponent's $2,000 bet into a $12,000 pot gave him about 6-1 odds by the time he called, an easy decision.

The turn brought an ace of diamonds, putting a flush draw on the board. Matros bet out to represent the nut flush draw, and when he was raised, he boldly came over the top by going all in. This is where reading the board to understand what the nuts are and knowing your opponent work in conjunction.

If Matros intended to represent the nut flush against a player who is considered to be a calling station, the nuance of his play likely would be missed. That type of player typically is willing to pay to see his set of queens beaten. But Matros knew his opponent was a professional, one who was capable of laying down big hands. He took his opponent's strength and made it a weakness.

Of course, there is another thing Matros had going for him: The WPT Championship was the biggest poker tournament in history, with a $25,000 buy-in and a top payout of more than $2.7 million. A professional (as opposed to an Internet qualifier, for instance) would prize the fame of having won the biggest poker event in the world the same way so many pros speak more of cherishing the World Series of Poker bracelet than the cash that goes with it. As a result, a pro such as Matros' opponent would have acute survival skills, especially early in an event. And you thought that knowing your opponent was just a matter of getting the name right.

♠ ♦ TOM McEVOY ♥ ♣

THE BEST THING THAT EVER HAPPENED TO TOM McEVOY? GETTING fired from his accounting job in Grand Rapids, Michigan. At the time, McEvoy was in his thirties and ready to try something new, namely a poker career. It was a pursuit he had been involved in since sitting across the kitchen table from his grandmother.

"I grew up playing penny-ante poker with her, starting when I was only five years old," McEvoy says. "Grandma used to beat the socks off me and my brothers. She taught all of us how to play, staked us to about $1 each, and then proceeded to win it back. It was either get better or keep losing to Grandma. We got better.

"In fact, my two brothers and I used to run our own poker games at our house. We played with each other, as well as the neighborhood kids. On more than one occasion, my mother would receive a phone call from an irate mother complaining about us McEvoy boys: 'Mrs. McEvoy, your sons have just taken my little Billy's allowance money in a poker game. What do you intend to do about it?'

"My mother usually replied along these lines: 'If your little Billy was stupid enough to play poker with my boys, he got exactly what he deserved.' Then she would chew us out for playing with little Billy and told us not to invite him back to any future games. About a week would go by and little Billy would apologize for his mother's phone call and beg us to let him back in the game."

Poker was not much more than a hobby when McEvoy completed college and began an accounting career in the late 1970s. But upon his dismissal several years later, and with no prospects for income, he headed back to Las Vegas to try his luck at the poker tables—despite the fact that he had never cleared more than $1,000 before. McEvoy won, and soon started flying back and forth from Michigan on a regular basis, before finally deciding to make the move and try it professionally.

"The tough part was convincing my wife, breaking the news to our three young children, telling parents and assorted friends and relatives, and most of all trying to convince everyone I had not lost my sanity," McEvoy says. Not only hadn't he lost his sanity, but four years later, McEvoy won the 1983 World Series of Poker championship.

The bespectacled, gray-haired McEvoy has also won three other WSOP titles and become a respected authority on the game. He has written or co-written more than ten books on poker strategy and has written a column for *Card Player* magazine since 1994.

McEvoy says that the best hand he ever played—"a hand that changed my life"—came during the $1,000 buy-in Limit Hold'em event at the 1983 World Series of Poker.

"I was deep in the tournament on the second and final day. The limits were $800-

$1600. The blinds were $200-$400. I raised in early position with pocket 7's, and got called by the big blind who has the A-J of hearts. The flop came 10 of spades, 5 of hearts, 4 of hearts. My opponent led out with a bet, and I raised him. I think that my 7's are probably the best hand, and he raised me back and I called."

The turn came a 10 of hearts, and McEvoy's opponent led out. McEvoy raised again, representing the heart flush that his opponent actually had. "He raised me back, and before I can call, the dealer burns and turns too quickly. The 2 of clubs came,

Early position: Generally considered one of the first three betting spots in any hand.

helping neither of us. Because I haven't acted yet, the floorman comes over and rules that I have the option of calling, raising, or folding, but that the deuce of clubs has to be returned to the deck, reshuffled in with the remaining cards and a new river card turned over.

"The pot has grown quite large because of my aggressive play, so I decide to gamble and call. The river card is a 7, making me a full house—7's full of 10's. My opponent is visibly shaken and I rake in a huge pot because of a dealer error that literally affected the rest of my life."

THE RAKE

There's no accounting for dealer error, just like there is no planning for luck. And there is not a poker book in the world that can strategize either. You can only hope that any time a dealer messes up, it helps you as well as it did Tom McEvoy.

As for McEvoy's actual strategy, it is instructive to note how he came in for a raise under the gun. Two things happen when you raise from first position: You are generally given credit for holding something strong, and if you can force players who do not have anything invested in the hand to fold, you have position on one or both of the blinds. That gives you the last move—one of the most powerful weapons in poker—and allows you to be more aggressive.

McEvoy raised on the flop to continue his aggressive approach. He called his opponent's re-raise, believing his 7's were the best hand with only one overcard on the board. McEvoy raised again after the 10 of hearts turned to pair the board and put hearts up. His opponent's re-raise told McEvoy he was likely facing a set of 10's or a flush, which might have prompted a lot of players to fold a middle pair.

But at some point in every tournament—sometimes at several points, no matter how tight you are playing—you will face a situation where you need to gamble. The large pot so deep in the tournament convinced McEvoy to take a chance on the river card from the reshuffled deck, and obviously it paid off.

This hand also serves as another example of the differences between limit and no-limit play. McEvoy never would have had that chance if that had been a No Limit tournament because his opponent would have likely moved all in on the turn when he made his flush, and it would have been impossible for McEvoy to call with a middle pair when facing a board showing paired 10's and a flush draw.

♠♦ CHRIS MONEYMAKER ♥♣

HERE IS WHAT YOU PROBABLY KNOW ABOUT CHRIS MONEYMAKER: He was a Nashville accountant who won a seat in the World Series of Poker world championship in an online tournament at PokerStars.com and beat the then-biggest field in poker history to collect a then-record $2.5 million.

Here is what you probably do not know about Chris Moneymaker: He tried to lose that online tournament. No lie.

"I had about sixty bucks in my account and I played a $40 two-table satellite on PokerStars one afternoon, just wasting time," Moneymaker explains. "I won it, which got me into a $600 tournament the next weekend. They were giving away three seats to the World Series, and fourth place was $8,000 in cash. I got down to the final table. I was the chip leader, and I was actually trying to dump my chips off to take fourth place and get the money. I didn't want the seat.

"My buddy called me out of the blue. He was watching from his computer in his apartment. He says, 'Man, what the fuck are you doing?' I said, 'I'm trying to get fourth place and get $8,000 in cash.' He told me he thought I was good enough to go out and play with those guys. I said, 'Man, you're insane. Those are the best in the world.'"

Here is something else you probably already know about Chris Moneymaker: He says the best hand he ever played came during his spectacular World Series championship run. Amazingly, though, it was not the hand at the final table where he bluffed Sam Farha into next year. Instead, he cites a hand that came the day before against Chuc Hoang.

"It was around seven o'clock in the evening. We were in our fourth two-hour session of the day, down to about thirty players, and I had been playing at the same table as Hoang for a couple hours. I don't think he got involved in more than a dozen hands in all that time. He struck me as a good player, but extremely conservative. He only plays if he has very strong hands.

"I was dealt A-3 of hearts. I had position on Hoang. He had made a strong raise, which I quickly called. No one else wanted in the hand. So it was just the two of us heads-up before the flop. I had built my stack up to about $700,000 after I had lost a hand to **Howard Lederer** earlier. Hoang had about half the same amount." The flop came 8-9-10 with no hearts and Hoang checked.

"I took that as a sign of weakness. I put him on A-K, actually. It made no sense that he was checking after betting so strong. I couldn't think what he might have. It was an interesting flop, but only if you had the hole cards to make it interesting.

"I checked too, which I thought would be an easy way to buy me some time to consider the turn and see what this guy might do next. The turn was a 6, after which Hoang bet $15,000—a weak bet at this stage of the tournament and at this stage of the hand. Really, it was a nothing bet considering our two stacks and his opening bet before the flop. I think he raised $30,000 pre-flop, so there was $60,000, and he bet $15,000 into the pot. I decided to raise him $15,000. Basically, it was a nothing raise, but I wanted to see where he was. I didn't have anything, so I wanted to see where I stood in the hand.

"I had no idea what kind of hand to put this guy on, but I didn't think it was strong. I was pretty sure he didn't have a 7 because he only checked after the flop. Plus, the way this guy had been playing, he wouldn't have raised pre-flop with a 7 unless it was pocket 7's.

"It was possible he had jack-something—J-A, J-Q, J-K. If he had J-Q, he'd have flopped a straight, and I would've been dead. But even these high cards didn't suggest such a soft bet on the turn. Once I raised the $15,000, I thought he would've come back with a lot of power.

"It was up to Hoang, and after an intermediate wait, he raised me another $15,000. I thought, Come on, this is ridiculous. He made it $15,000, then I raised $15,000, and he came back with $15,000. I was about ready to fold when I decided I was pretty tired and I wanted to see where this guy is, so I re-raised $100,000.

"My thinking when I made the play was, if he doesn't have a 7, he's going to lay it down and I'm going to take this pot. The move took me down to about $500,000 in chips. If he had called, he'd be down to approximately $180,000. So he thought about it forever, and finally, when he looked like he was ready to fold, he said in a very soft voice, 'I'm going to pay you off.'

"Those were probably the worst words I'd ever heard. Hoang was basically throwing in the towel, but actually decided to play it instead. I thought, aw, crap. I've basically got no outs. If an ace or a king comes, it's probably going to hit his hand. I don't know what he could be drawing at. He has to have something in that range. I'm screwed."

Hoang called the $100,000. The river brought a jack, which was no help to Moneymaker. "I'm dead in the hand. I've got no chance. Hoang checked, and for the life of me, I don't know why, but I decided what the heck, I'm going to move all in because I just don't think he has it.

"Hoang thought about it for another month, it seemed like. He sat there, and I stared off into space while he thought, and he finally decided to lay it down. He said, 'My 7's no good,' and he showed me a 7. He had a straight. I flipped up my A-3 of hearts.

"He had played about twelve hands in the whole day I'd played with him. I wanted to send a message of, 'Don't mess with me. Stay out of my pots.' Also, I wanted to rattle him, make him play. He'd been sitting there milking everything. He went out the next hand.

"I consider it my greatest hand because I had the balls to keep going at him. I thought I had him on a really good read. But my read was actually completely wrong. It goes to show you that a read doesn't always have to be right. You just have to have the heart to put your money in there and go for it. I took three shots at it. I fired three bullets at the pot, and it took that last big bullet.

"The hand gave me chips, then when I showed the A-3, I looked around the table and

I could almost see the fear of God in people's eyes, like, 'Oh, my god, what a play.' There were two people, and you could see they just didn't believe it. For the next forty-five minutes, I pretty much ran the table. I got to control the table any way I wanted to."

THE RAKE

When you win a pot with a bluff—especially when you do it with two cards you probably should not even call with and do it against a tight player who never bets unless he has the nuts or close, and fire three big shots at the pot, including all in—then you get to run the table for the rest of the night.

The value that Chris Moneymaker got from his gutsy play was not just building his stack back up to around $1 million, but also the fear he put into the rest of the table. He could play any two cards from any position, while his opponents found themselves raising their standards for hands they dared open with.

Moneymaker had not played a hand against Chuc Hoang when this one came up, so he had no history. In those cases, players rely on reputation and betting patterns. When a tight player such a Hoang made a pre-flop raise of $30,000, Moneymaker immediately put him on A-K because those are the types of hands that tight players play.

Hoang's check on the 8-9-10 flop likely meant one of two things: He had the nut straight and was trying to trap, or it had missed him completely. Moneymaker read Hoang's check as weakness because most tight players will bet out to take the pot down immediately if they have made their hand.

Semi-bluff: Betting out or raising when you have some kind of hand, but not as big as you are making it appear. It's not a total bluff because you still have some outs that would allow you to win the pot. **Lay down:** To fold a hand.

When the turn brought a 6, a gutshot straight was on board. Hoang bet $15,000, an underbet to the bigger pot, which told Moneymaker that Hoang wasn't declaring the strength of his hand as much as he was stating how much he was willing to lose.

That is when Moneymaker began executing the bluffer's blueprint. He raised Hoang the amount of Hoang's bet, if only to establish how much he liked his hand. Then, when Hoang re-raised him the same amount—the same, small amount, by comparison—Moneymaker stepped up the assault by coming over the top for $100,000.

Hoang called, which was the wrong play because he had the best hand. In fact, it was the wrong move even if he had the worst hand, and here's why: Once Hoang called, he was pot-committed. He would still face a decision on the river, and even if he folded the way he eventually would, he would not have enough chips to play his way back into contention without some miracle double-ups.

So if Hoang was going to call Moneymaker's big raise on the turn, he would have been better off moving all in and putting the pressure on Moneymaker. Hoang had a straight, even if it was the small end of the straight, so he had more than a semi-bluff working. What's more, Hoang should have been able to see that Moneymaker had a half-million-dollar stack that would have made it easy for him to lay down his hand and still feel confident he had chips to play with.

In all, Moneymaker took three shots at the pot. When you are bluff-committed and have assumed the aggressive lead each time, your opponents do not know whether you have the nuts or nothing, but playing power poker—and in this case, the power of Moneymaker's bigger stack—usually wins you the pot.

The key play here, other than Hoang's call, was Moneymaker's all in on the river. If he does not bet, there is no way he can win the hand. The same goes if he makes a bet for anything less than one for Hoang's tournament life.

One final point about this hand: It is exactly the kind of bold move you must learn to make when you are down to the last few tables of a tournament because tight play only gets you so far. Big moves win you the chips to win the event because the end game is much more about bluffing. This move would not have worked in your basic home game of Limit Hold'em because both players would have had so much money already invested in the pot that the odds demanded a call of any bet.

♠♦ DANIEL NEGREANU ♥♣

YOU COULD MAKE A CASE THAT DANIEL NEGREANU IS THE BEST TOURNAMENT POKER player in the game today. He was named Player of the Year at the 2004 World Series of Poker, cashing six times and winning his third bracelet in the $2,000 buy-in Limit Hold'em event. He followed that performance by winning the Championship Poker at the Plaza No Limit Hold'em tournament. And followed that by winning the World Poker Tour event at the Borgata. Any way you look at it, it is an impressive hat trick for the Toronto-born Negreanu, who first gained distinction by wearing hockey jerseys at the table until his then-fiancée Zambonied his wardrobe.

While the thirty-one-year-old Negreanu appears very mild-mannered and proper—his mother still regularly packs his lunch in a brown paper bag, after all—he often speaks of how poker fulfills his competitive desire, not to mention his antiauthority streak. "I can be my own boss," he says, admitting he considers side games "work" but pointing out that he also gets to set his own hours. "What could be better than that?"

The best hand Negreanu ever played came heads-up against **Freddy Deeb** at the final table of the Championship Poker at the Plaza event in 2004.

"Freddy and I have played a lot in the cash games, but we'd never played heads up before. I was really looking forward to the match because I felt as though we had very similar styles. Both of us like to play a lot of hands and see a lot of flops.

"With the blinds at just $800-$1,600 with a $200 ante, Freddy had $342,300 to my $337,700. That's over 200 big bets each. This wasn't going to be raise-it-and-take-it poker."

Negreanu drew an A-7 offsuit and limped from the button. In the big blind, Deeb raised $7,000. "Now, we hadn't been doing that, so I assumed that Freddy must have had a pretty strong hand. With an ace and position though, I wasn't about to let him take the pot right there, so I called.

"The flop came king of spades, 6 of hearts, 2 of hearts, and Freddy fired out $16,000, which represented close to a pot-size bet. I had position and I had a key card, the ace of hearts. Also, if Freddy had a hand like Q-Q or J-J, that king on the board may freeze him on the turn, at which time I could pick up the pot. It was too early to make my move on the flop, so I decided to wait for the turn and see what developed. The turn was the 4 of spades and Freddy checked, as I'd hoped he would.

"Now I have to make one thing clear: The 4 of spades is a scare card. Freddy and I both like the 'little cards.' That's no secret to either of us. Freddy knows I could have made a straight with 3-5, two pair with 6-4, or some other off-the-wall hand. So I feel like Freddy has something like J-J and if I bet it strongly on the turn and river, he would let those jacks go. I bet $30,000. Freddy called and now I was going over how much I was going to bluff on the river. 'One hundred twenty thousand. That's a big-size bet that won't break me,' I thought.

"The river came the 4 of hearts. All that card did was make me a fake flush. Now this is where the hand gets kind of crazy. I was fully expecting Freddy to check and I had my $120,000 cocked and ready to fire. Then Freddy comes out betting $65,000!

"That bet was so odd to me, though. How can he bet that card, I thought. I know he didn't make the nut flush because I have the ace of hearts. I don't think that card made him a full house because he probably would have raised me on the turn with two pair or a set.

"Before I decided what I wanted to do, I just wanted to try to figure out what Freddy had. So I went back to all the clues: He raised before the flop out of position and that felt like strength to me since it was so rare; he bet big on the flop to protect his hand; and he didn't like that straight card on the turn, but he also didn't fold.

"Aha, okay, so he has A-K. Never mind how I know that. So if he has A-K, then why would he bet the river when such a scary card came? Oh, I know, I know! He bet that scary card for two reasons: 1) He was hoping I would call him with a worse king but felt like I would check a worse king behind him, and 2) he knew I couldn't raise him on the river unless I made a very strong hand.

Fake flush: Holding four cards to a flush when there are no common cards left to come. **Big bet:** In a Limit game, it is the size of the bet on the last two rounds; in a No Limit game, it is the size of the big blind.

"Feeling like he had A-K, I knew he couldn't possibly call a raise on the river. After finally building up the courage, I decided I needed to make a play at this pot. I raised $100,000 more.

"Freddy deliberated for a little while and finally said, 'You must have flopped a set.' I, of course, said nothing, being the shy, quiet guy that I am. Then Freddy's hand went into the muck. Ever feel like you have a really big secret and are dying to tell someone? That's how I felt at that moment. 'If I show a bluff, is that good for the game?' I asked.

"'Yeah, sure,' replied Freddy.

"'All right, then that must be good for the game!' I said as I turned my cards faceup and raked in the monster pot. I just don't know if there is a better feeling than that."

THE RAKE

This might be one of the greatest bluff hands of all time when it comes to putting an opponent on a hand and strategically betting to run that opponent off that hand. Negreanu won't say how he deduced that Deeb had exactly A-K—he is not giving away the whole game plan here—but the way he recounted the dynamics of the betting at least provides a blueprint for narrowing the range of hands an opponent has.

But first, let's start with Negreanu's pre-flop limp with A-7. Many people want to raise automatically with any kind of ace, but Negreanu and many great players limp with ace-rag because it doesn't play well after the flop. If you hit your ace, you have a weak kicker, and if you don't hit it and bet out after your pre-flop raise, it is likely that the flop that missed you altogether hit someone else and that you will probably get called, giving you more trouble down the line.

Another key part of Negreanu's play was knowing his own reputation, specifically as someone who will play small cards. And he knew that Deeb knew it too. So when the 4 came on the turn, he bet it because it played to his table image.

What's more, Negreanu was willing to bet strongly on the turn and the river for two reasons: First, the top players have the heart to carry out a bluff in a big way, especially against an opponent who is good enough to lay down big hands; and second, he knew that his opponent liked to play small-bet poker and would be uncomfortable with big-bet poker.

Then, after recapping Deeb's betting pattern to believe he was up against A-K and determining he was going to make one last play, Negreanu had to find the right amount to raise Deeb's $65,000 bet on the river. He chose to go with $100,000 because it was an amount that looked like he wanted Deeb to call and bet into a trap. If Deeb had called, Negreanu would have been down about 4-1 in chips and still believed he would have had enough ammunition to come back and win.

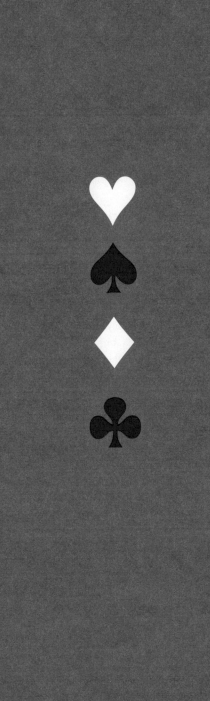

♠ ◆ EVELYN NG ♥ ♣

WOMEN SITTING DOWN AT THE POKER TABLE USED TO BE A RARITY. It was a man's world, and they had the unsavory reputations and smoke-scented clothes to prove it. But that has all changed today. Whether you're talking cash games or tournaments, women regularly ante up. The growing number of women players has made the issue almost moot.

What hasn't changed, however, is the way some men underestimate women players. Some play softer against women, shying away from raising them the way they ordinarily would play back at men. Others simply don't give women credit for having a hand.

Some would also admit that the more attractive the woman, the greater the advantage she has. If so, then one of the many women who figure to benefit from that kind of male chauvinism is Evelyn Ng.

A poker pro for more nearly a decade, the 5'11" beauty went from the pool halls of her native Toronto to the casino, first dealing blackjack, then poker.

"I saw the same people winning all the time," Ng says, "so I knew it was a game of skill and I knew it was something that I could learn. I paid attention when I was dealing. I bought some books. Then I started playing a year after I started dealing, and I was winning from the first day."

When she turned twenty-one, Ng was taken to Las Vegas by good friend and fellow Torontonian **Daniel Negreanu**, whom she dated when she was younger. (Ng once famously lost a hand to Negreanu when they dated and kicked him in the shins afterward. Hey, some people take losing hard.) "I stayed for a week," Ng says. "Then I came back a few weeks later and stayed for about five months. I was playing $10-$20 when I first came out. In Toronto, poker was relatively new. It was underground, then it became more public. I didn't see people playing for a living in Toronto. But when I came to Vegas, there were tons of people who were playing poker for a living even at $5-$10 limits and even lower. I couldn't believe it."

So she joined them, although that did not go over particularly well with Mom and Dad back in Toronto. "They hated it," Ng says. "They were more worried because with Asian families, everybody knows of their one cousin or one uncle who squandered away the whole family fortune or something. Or they probably envisioned me hanging out with mobsters. So they weren't too thrilled with it. But after a couple years, they saw how well I was doing and I showed them my records and I tried to help out with things around the house, so they became more accepting."

Ng made a living in cash games, then began playing tournaments. In 2003, she finished second to Clonie Gowen in the World Poker Tour's Ladies Night one-table event. In 2004, she cashed in a World Series of Poker No-Limit Hold'em event and placed in the top seven twice at the Ultimate Poker Challenge.

"I love the competition," Ng says. "I did like to gamble a lot. But now that I play poker for a living, I don't consider myself a gambler. It's almost like being a stockbroker. There is an element of gamble to it, but it's really a sure thing if you know what you're doing."

Ng gained confidence to believe she knew what she was doing in poker in the 2003 World Poker Open in Tunica, Mississippi, in the best hand she ever played.

"I was new to tournaments. It was my second one, I think. I was involved in a hand where I had raised with two jacks and I got three-bet by someone I know is a solid player and I know perceives me to be a solid player in tournaments. He three-bet me, so I knew he had a very big hand."

The flop came an ace with two small cards. Ng checked and her opponent made a good-size bet. "But for some reason I thought the only way he would three-bet me is if he had a big pocket pair. With the ace on board, the chances of him having pocket aces weren't very good, so I figured he had pocket kings. I check-raised him all my chips all in.

Three-bet: A term used in Limit games; a player makes a bet, another player raises, thus making it two bets to play, then a third player re-raises, making it three bets to continue.

"He said, 'If you have two queens, you're the best player in the world,' and he mucked the two kings faceup. I said, 'Yeah, I had an ace.' I didn't want to tell him the truth.

"That hand gave me a lot of courage to make a move without actually having a hand. Before, I would've just said, 'Oh, well, I missed. I fold.' But I realized I had the courage and the ability to take a pot that I didn't deserve.

"It's a lot of fun. Those chips won off a bluff are like the sweetest chips you can get."

THE RAKE

Once again, Ng's knowledge of her opponent was crucial to this hand. Ng knew she was up against a solid player, and she also knew her opponent viewed her the same way. But here's the thing about solid players: They have the discipline to fold big hands when their tournament lives are at stake.

If Ng had not had a read on her opponent's style, or if she knew he was an all-or-nothing player, she indeed might have folded a dangerous hand such as jacks—dangerous because they're big enough picture cards to entice you into a pot and small enough picture cards to get you wiped out.

But Ng elected to play the hand, and play it big, after she reviewed the betting. If her opponent indeed had a big pocket pair, as his re-raise pre-flop indicated, it was unlikely to be aces once an ace flopped because most players bet a set of aces passively in order to trap an opponent. If her opponent in fact had aces, he would have had the best hand and would have wanted Ng to catch something on the turn or the river that would prompt her to bet at the pot.

So when Ng's opponent made a sizable bet, he was helping her narrow down the kinds of hands he might have, and she felt comfortable ruling out aces because there was one on the board.

Then came the risk. Ng determined she had the worse hand, but she knew she could represent the better hand with a check-raise all in and an ace on board that could match the one she acted like she had in her hand.

What's more, she believed her table image gave her some credit with her opponent that she would not be bluffing with nothing. These kinds of situations happen every day at every poker table—in tournaments they frequently determine who survives and who dies—and it is worth repeating that this hand gave Ng the confidence after making a big move against a good player when she did not have the best hand.

♠♦ MEN "THE MASTER" NGUYEN ♥♣

THREE DECADES AGO, LONG BEFORE HE WOULD GAIN THE NICKNAME THE MASTER AND become one of the most successful and boisterous characters in big-time poker, Men Nguyen was escaping war-torn South Vietnam in a boat. Even a life-threatening voyage, he believed, was better than living under communist rule.

"It was terrible, leaving my father and mother and brothers and sisters," Nguyen recalls. "I was on the boat and I looked back crying and thinking I'd never come back to the country. I was twenty-two.

"It took five nights and four days to go from Vietnam to Malaysia. Each day, we had a little sip of water and some rice. That was all. We had eighty-eight people, forty of them were kids. We didn't have a compass to know where to go. We looked at the sunrise. That's where we went."

Finally, they spotted Malaysia and dreamed of freedom. But coming ashore would prove to be as difficult as the first part of the journey already had been. Nguyen says Malaysian officials refused to accept people seeking refugee status if they entered the country in a boat.

"So, we had to wreck the boat and jump into the water and they'd rescue us," Nguyen says. "We pushed the kids to land on the little boat we had. And we destroyed the big boat." At last, Nguyen and his fellow refugees had found safe harbor. But his next goal was to reach the United States. There, he had an ace in the hole.

"My father fought against the communists, protecting the South against the North," Nguyen explains. "Before I left, my father said, 'It might help you if you tell the embassy [in Malaysia] that your father fought with the Americans against North Vietnam.' So I told them my father was in the army. It worked."

A sponsor brought Nguyen to the United States in the mid- to late-'70s. He was placed in Los Angeles, unable to speak a word of English. "I went to school, then my friend offered me a job delivering furniture," the 5'4" Nguyen remembers. "It was a heavy job. I had to carry a sofa and a love seat upstairs. But I'd take any job in this country to survive. I got ten bucks a day, two dollars an hour."

By 1978, Nguyen says he got a job as a machinist making $4 an hour. "A year later, I made seven bucks an hour," Nguyen says with his well-known laugh. "I learn fast." Unfortunately, he also learned about heartbreak.

"I met a girl in school and got married," Nguyen says. "I had a kid with her and then she left. She took my kid and left. I was very sad. I was lovesick and had nobody in this country. I almost killed myself. I had a gun. But I said I wouldn't die for the lady."

A friend who was helping Nguyen work through his emotional distress took him on a junket to Caesars Palace in Las Vegas. Nguyen played most of the casino games before he found the poker room. "God pointed Men to the poker room," Nguyen says. "They played Five-Card Stud like in my country."

They played it better than in his country, as it turned out. "The first time I played, I played $15-$30 and lost $3,200, twenty years ago," Nguyen says. "But I loved the game. The next week, I came back. I won $1,600."

By now, Nguyen was running several dry-cleaning shops. Hooked on the game, he was working from early morning until the evening, then heading to the Bicycle Club Casino, to learn some expensive lessons.

They paid off. Coming onto the poker scene in the late 1980s, the man they now call The Master started cashing enough to quit his day job and devote himself full-time to poker. (As for the wonderful moniker, Nguyen says he was first called The Master by a poker student, and he liked it—who wouldn't?—so he kept it.) Nguyen has since gone on to win six World Series of Poker bracelets in such varied games as Seven Card Stud, Limit Hold'em, Omaha 8-or-Better, and Ace-to-5 Triple Draw Lowball.

The Master says the best hand he ever played came during the World Poker Tour's event at the Borgata in 2004. "It was very late, around one in the morning. The tournament had about five tables left. I knew this guy didn't have a hand, but he had me beat for sure. The blinds were $3,000-$6,000, and the antes were $300. He had about $80,000 in chips. I had about $75,000."

Ace-to-5 Triple Draw Lowball: A five-card game in which you try to make the best low hand–in this case A-2-3-4-5–and get to draw up to three times, with betting on each round.

The player under the gun raised with pocket 10's. Nguyen held A-K in the big blind. "I knew if I pounded him back, he is going to go all in because he has a pair of 10's and I have A-K. He raised me $10,000 and I called him. I didn't re-raise him to make sure I could see the flop.

"The flop came J-5-2, one club. I checked. Of course he was going to bet to see where I am. He bet $12,000, a little bit more than the original raise. I know he doesn't have a jack. Why? Because he raised before the flop. He might have A-K, A-Q, but A-J is very rare to raise under the gun.

"I represented a jack or a big hand before the flop and I call his $12,000 and raise him $40,000 more. He showed me the two 10's and mucked it.

"That's the greatest play because you put the guy on the same hand as you and he cannot call you except if he has aces, kings, or queens. I like the hand where you play against the other guy and he doesn't have a hand and you pound him so he lays it down. You create the bigger hand to play against the guy and pound him."

THE RAKE

This sequence is a prime example of the way the best players in the world don't play their own hands as much as they play their opponents'. Sure, Men Nguyen played his hole cards to start—he had to see if he wanted to enter the pot at all—but after that he played the board and his opponent's hand, essentially showing the skill and artistry that has made No Limit Hold'em an addictive pastime.

Nguyen represented a big hand before the flop by calling the $10,000 raise. Granted, he did have one, but the key is that he did not give away any information as to just how strong it was by re-raising his opponent. This move gave him the possibility of bluffing at the pot if he didn't catch anything on the flop, because his opponent would not have been able to put him on a hand.

When the flop came J-5-2, Nguyen was able to narrow down the range of hands his opponent likely was holding because it is rare that someone raises pre-flop with A-J, so the jack-high flop probably didn't improve his opponent's hand.

When Nguyen check-raised for more than half of his stack on the flop, he was representing an even bigger hand—aces, kings, queens, or even jacks—and pressured his opponent into laying down a pocket pair. This is one of the most basic philosophies of poker: When you bet out, you have two ways to win—by having the best hand or by having your opponent fold. If you check, you have only one way to win—by having the best hand.

♠ ♦ SCOTTY NGUYEN ♥ ♣

SCOTTY NGUYEN IS A GOOD TIME, BABY. HE SAUNTERS IN AND OUT OF A POKER ROOM, wearing multicolored sunglasses and medallions jangling around his neck. The look says "good time to follow" more than "too cool for the room." Nguyen is vocal and playful at the table, sometimes chatting up opponents as a strategic ploy to find out how comfortable they are with their hands, sometimes due to his natural ebullience. And Nguyen never seems to be without a beer—something many players avoid, but it fits his aggressive-playing and outsize personality.

And when you've won four World Series of Poker bracelets, including one for the main event, along with ranking as one of the biggest money-winners in poker tournament history, well, why wouldn't you be a good time, baby?

Especially when you consider how he got there. The forty-four-year-old Nguyen was born in Vietnam but says fled when he was eleven, along with his nine-year-old brother. "My mom sold just about everything in the house to put the money together so we could leave," Nguyen says. "You have to pay somebody to let you get on the boat to escape.

"We landed in Taiwan for two years. Then from Taiwan, an American sponsored me to come over here. That's the way it is. When you're in the refugee camps and underage, they put your name on the list. It goes all over the world, not just America."

The American family that picked Nguyen also gave him his name—Thuan Nguyen. "That's my real name—Thuan Nguyen," he says. "Thuan means 'peaceful.'"

Nice name. Good message. Not so easy to pronounce. "My boss said they couldn't call me by my given name because it was too easy to mispronounce," Nguyen says, "so he said, 'We'll call you Scotty.'"

It was while working in a casino in the late 1980s that Nguyen would stand for hours and watch people play poker. That's how he taught himself the game, and once he sat down, he found he had a knack for it.

Now a wildly successful poker champion in America, Nguyen has not forgotten where he came from. He bought his mother one of the biggest houses in the Las Vegas area and does whatever he can financially to support his extended family in Vietnam. A good man, who says the best hand he ever played came on the final hand of the 1998 World Series of Poker championship.

"I had J-9. I raised every hand because I had a big chip lead. This guy was so scared. He'd call me with A-Q, A-K, and I'd raise him with 10-2, 10-J, and he'd let me get there.

He didn't re-raise and make me muck my hand. He'd let me see the flop. When I'd see the flop, it was so hard for him to outplay me."

In this hand, Nguyen raised with J-9 offsuit. His opponent had Q-10 of hearts. The flop came 9-9-8, rainbow. Nguyen flopped three 9's. His opponent had an inside straight draw and two overcards. Nguyen checked, and his opponent bet $100,000. Nguyen called.

The turn came an 8 of hearts for a board of 9-9-8-8. Nguyen filled up, 9's over 8's. His opponent now had an inside straight flush draw. Nguyen checked. His opponent bet another $100,000. The river came an 8 of spades, putting a full house on the board. Nguyen bet $310,000 to put his opponent all in if he called. "He's thinking, thinking, thinking. He almost folded, and I look at him and I say, 'If you call me, baby, it's going to be all over.' He said, 'I call.'"

"He threw his hand in the muck. No one saw it. They only saw my hand—the winning hand. I turned over 9's full. He walked over to me and said, 'Scotty, I knew sooner or later you were going to get me, so why not just call you now?'

"That was my greatest hand because that's the hand I won the World Series with. That's the hand I remember. That's the hand that made me become somebody from a nobody. Now people recognize who I am."

THE RAKE

The trademark aggressive play that got Nguyen to the final table also earned him the world championship when he went heads-up. He was raising every hand, no matter his holdings, putting pressure on his opponent and testing his heart. When you give action like that, you force your opponents to make a stand and try to play back at you. When Nguyen's opponent in this hand finally did that, Nguyen had a big hand.

But the key to this hand was the way Nguyen changed his betting approach on the flop and the turn. He became a caller, not a raiser. When he flopped three 9's, Nguyen played a strong hand as weak by checking and calling. That is when he began thinking to the river about how he would induce his opponent to push in all his chips.

When the turn came an 8, giving Nguyen a full house, he checked and called again, once more acting weak. By the time the river fell and Nguyen moved all in, his opponent was committed, perhaps hoping he could play the board that read 8's full and split the pot. But by then it was too late: Nguyen had milked the last of his opponent's stack.

♠♦ PAUL PHILLIPS ♥♣

YOU NEVER KNOW WHAT LOOK YOU WILL GET WITH PAUL PHILLIPS.
He might show up at the table wearing a T-shirt and jeans, or he might don a suit. More notable, however, are his hair choices. They have ranged from dark and long with a bushy beard to close-cropped and magenta. Or orange.

Despite his chameleon-like tendencies, with Phillips one thing is certain: He is a terrific tournament player. He began playing casually in 1994 while gaining a reputation as a software programming whiz. Five years later, when he cashed out of the high-tech bubble for millions, he began competing in big-time poker tournaments.

In 2001, Phillips came in first in a $1,000 buy-in No Limit Hold'em tournament at Commerce Casino then less than a week later, he took second in the $5,000 buy-in main event. Later that year, Phillips made some comments about the prize pool distribution at the World Series of Poker. He believed his remarks were lightly critical. Binion's Horseshoe officials, the hosts of the tournament, disagreed and promptly barred Phillips from subsequent events. Eventually, they relented, and Phillips was allowed to compete in the main event, and in a turn of events that characterized his WSOP experience in 2001, Phillips lost his $170,000 stack when he drew pocket aces in consecutive hands and had them cracked both times.

Phillips would recover nicely, though, finishing second in tournament winnings to eventual World Series of Poker champion **Chris Moneymaker** in 2003. He closed that year by winning the $10,000 buy-in Five Diamond World Poker Classic No-Limit Hold'em championship, thus joining a select group of players to have won a million dollars in an event outside the World Series of Poker. But Phillips says the best hand he ever played came earlier in 2003 at the No Limit Hold'em Championship at the Borgata.

"Money was very deep and the blinds were only $25-$50. A couple of people limped in front of me, including Huck Seed, and I made it $400. **Jennifer Harman** called and Huck Seed calls. I have two black aces."

The flop came 2-3-6, with two clubs. Harman checked, and Seed bet $600. Phillips called and Harman folded. The turn was an offsuit 9, and Seed bet out again.

"What I'm doing here is trying to look like I'm on a flush draw, which is very plausible because I have the ace of clubs, so I know he's not on a flush draw. I just called him again.

"Now the river was an offsuit 4, so the board was 2-3-6-4-9—meaning any 5 makes a straight—so any set had me beat, any two pair, a million hands have me beat. Huck moved all in.

"I almost instantly call him with the aces, and he has J-10 offsuit—no hand, no draw, just bluffing the whole way, and I busted him the second hand of this thing. The funny thing about that story is, we also busted a guy on the first hand of the tournament. A giant buy-in tournament, and we busted people on the first two hands."

THE RAKE

To understand the significance of this seemingly simple hand, you first have to remember that Huck Seed was a former world champion. He is enshrined in The Horseshoe's Gallery of Champions for his 1996 victory. And he made the kind of moves in this hand that you would expect of a world champion.

Understand, too, that if you can identify what a champion does, then you can take that strength and make it a weakness. Seed's big bet on the flop and his even bigger all in so early in a tournament—the second hand, after all—is an extreme example of a regular play. A great player often knocks another great player off a hand because the second player is capable of folding, which is part of the first player's arsenal. This is part of the great artistry of No Limit Hold'em.

The difference here is that Phillips saw Seed coming. It was one of those classic he-knows-that-I-know-that-he-knows-that-I-know situations. Phillips knew that the basis of Seed's play was putting all the pressure on Phillips to call with a mere pair, even a pair of aces, against a highly coordinated board. It is an impossible call.

Coordinated board: The common cards work strongly in various combinations to make a hand, say a straight, a flush, or a full house, or some combination of the three.

But Phillips also knew that Seed easily could make this move without a hand—and probably *was* making the move without a hand—so he made the call. This, too, is part of the greater artistry of No Limit Hold'em, a brilliant execution of the commandment "Know Thy Opponent."

♠♦ THOMAS "AMARILLO SLIM" PRESTON ♥♣

"I'VE BEEN OLD FOR A HUNDRED YEARS," SAYS THE WORLD'S MOST FAMOUS POKER player, and you bet he's from Amarillo, Texas. "Our population's been the same the last thirty years. Never varies. Every time some woman gets pregnant, some man leaves town."

Born Thomas Preston, Slim was poker's first major showman—he even hosted *Amarillo Slim's Super Bowl of Poker* in the 1980s—and there are now plans to depict his life story in a film with Nicolas Cage. The seventy-six-year-old legend, who still thinks of himself as an "ol' cowboy," started playing poker more than fifty years ago and has never lost his passion for anteing up.

"I still go to all the major tournaments," Slim says. "But I don't go stay a month like a lot of people do. I've got nothing to prove.

"I've hung up a shingle for thirty-two years now that I'd play anybody in the world. Thankfully I still get several people who want to play.

"I played two at The Victoria [in London]. I went to the Aviation [Club in Paris]. I went to Baden-Baden and played two guys there. Then I went to Moscow, played one man, went to Leningrad and played one, went to Vienna and represented America in a world tournament. All in one trip. They'd rather beat me for $3 than beat someone else for $3,000. Their objective is to beat me at one pot.

"You remember when you're little and you played tag? Well I'm always 'it.'"

Slim says the best hand he ever played—"the most satisfaction I ever got"—came in a high-profile heads-up match in the mid-1970s.

"As far as I'm concerned, the best woman poker player in the world is named Betty Carey. She had played **Doyle Brunson** heads-up and she beat him. She played Sam Petrillo and she beat him. She played Billy Baxter. She played about seven or eight guys—I'm talking about the top players—and she beat 'em.

"One day, Betty called me at home and she says, 'Slim, I'm ready to graduate.' Well, I just knew of her. We weren't well acquainted. I said, 'Ready to graduate?' She said, 'Yes, you're my next victim.' I said, 'Betty, you'd better leave well enough alone because what you smell cookin' isn't on the fire.'

"I think that got her a little excited, so she posted her money—$100,000—and I played her at the Las Vegas Hilton. They roped us off. We both showed up on time, and they're getting chips and they're getting cards and dealers. Well, I drink coffee. I'm an undrinking stiff. I always thought liquor was made to sell, not to drink. I don't use it. But I love my opponents to use it.

"Anyway, I said, 'Betty, I'm going to order some coffee. Would you like something?'

She said, 'Yes, you know I believe I would. I'd like to have some hot tea.' Now, no one in that room except one person knew what was happening. They didn't even have a clue that there was something wrong with what I'm saying.

"Anyway, they went and got this tea. So, here come the chips and they're counting out a couple hundred thousand worth, and I know that she's relaxed and she's not thinking about our game. So, as she takes a sip and sets it back down, I say to her, 'Betty, how's your tea?'

"'Oh, this is excellent tea. Very good. Thank you, Slim. That was kind of you.'

"We started play, and about fifteen minutes later a pot comes up that a show dog couldn't jump over. This thing's in Technicolor. It started off mediocre and it ended up a whale.

"I had twenty-some-odd thousand, and she moved in on me. I didn't have a hand. I say to Betty, 'Betty, how do you like your hand?'

"She says, 'Slim, this is a real good hand.' But that's not what she said when I asked her about that tea. She was sincere about how she liked her tea. Follow me? Now I know this gal's lying to me. I look at her, and she looks like she couldn't swallow boiled okra because she didn't have a hand.

"Everybody's yapping and listening and looking. I had two 6's. That wouldn't beat anything. So I called her, and, man, you could hear a mouse press on cotton. It got just as quiet in that room. She says, 'Take it.' I said, 'I'd be glad to take it.' She said, 'Oh, you got a couple of pairs or something?' I said, 'No, I only got two 6's,' and let me tell you, that room exploded. She had nothing."

THE RAKE

If ever there was a perfect poker story about discovering a tell, this is it. Slim got all the information he needed from the only other person playing the game.

With Slim, the game began before the game began. He found a moment when his opponent was relaxed and unconcerned with what would take place. Betty Carey's sincere and calm tone when she was drinking the tea that Slim had so thoughtfully provided betrayed her when Slim was trying to decide whether to call her.

Slim probably couldn't get away with such talk these days. Strict enforcement of Tournament Directors Association rules forbids talking about hands if it is meant to induce action. But years ago, out talking an opponent was as much a part of the game as outplaying one. And of course, it's still part of any friendly home game.

Even so, players give off tells not only in their voices but also in the way they sit, the way they act, the way they bet, check, raise, and riffle chips. That's why players wear sunglasses and hats, and even cover their mouths while waiting for an opponent to respond to a bet. That's also why players work on examining the kind of tells they give off with every movement and, further, work to create false tells to play into the deception that is poker.

"That's people," Slim says. "That's psychology. In a moment when it doesn't pertain to the game, people will tell the truth. In poker, even if I say, 'You got something?' Well, it's a damn cinch you're going to lie. If you have it, you're going to lie, and if you don't have it, you're going to lie. I knocked it off like a dead lamb. I just knew this gal was running without the ball."

♠♦ GREG RAYMER ♥♣

HE BECAME KNOWN AS FOSSILMAN, BUT HE REPRESENTED EVERYMAN, AND in 2004, he won everything—every bit of the $5 million that went to the winner of the World Series of Poker championship. Not bad for an Internet qualifier.

In the biggest event in the history of poker—nearly 2,600 entrants—Greg Raymer, a patent attorney from Stonington, Connecticut, stormed to the final table of the $10,000 buy-in event with more than $8 million in chips and proceeded to run over the competition until he collected every last one, finally busting **David Williams** in heads-up play.

Known as Fossilman for his use of actual fossils as card protectors at the table—after the tournament, he interested more than a few players in buying some—Raymer was also best known for his cheesy green, lizard-eyed glasses, bought at the Tower of Terror at Disney World during a family vacation.

When Raymer decided to play a hand, he would make his bet, then sport the reptile specs to stare down opponents—or give them headaches—and prevent them from picking up tells.

As you might expect from a new multimillionaire, the forty-year-old Raymer (who was a regular at Foxwoods Resort Casino even before his magnificent World Series) has since left law to play poker full-time.

Fittingly, the 2004 champion says the best hand he ever played came during his championship charge, but it was not at the final table. Instead, the hand came with about fifty players remaining against Danish pro **Marcel Luske.**

"The important part of this hand is not so much what I had. What I like about this hand is that I came up with a plan before I looked at my cards. Marcel is very active. He plays lots of hands. Sometimes he'll have relatively junky hands—small suited connectors, one-gappers, hands with which you usually can't call a big re-raise. But he'll also open the same way with a big hand."

With blinds at $5,000-$10,000, Luske open-raised for $30,000. Raymer's stack was $250,000-$300,000. "He opened this pot from early position, and for whatever reason, I feel he has a pretty decent hand. Nothing I can pin down. It could have been random chance that I felt that way.

"There were about four or five players in between us, and while I was waiting for them to act, I'm thinking to myself, 'If I look down and see A-A or K-K, instead of just making a pot-size raise, which would've been maybe a third of my stack, I thought I'd push in for $300,000.'

"But what I'm going to do is if I look down [and see one of those hands], then really fast with kind of a caveman grunt, I'm going to push all in. Then I'm going to sit there really, really passive, so it's going to look like a scripted play, and it *is* scripted.

"That way, he's going to say, 'That looked scripted; he just decided to re-raise me no matter what.' So if he has A-10 or K-Q or some decent hand, he's going to call.

"I looked down. I did happen to find aces. I did the caveman grunt. And then sat there. It actually took quite a while, but he called with A-K."

The flop came Q-Q-small card. Luske needed to catch a running J-10 or running K-K to win. His cards did not come, and Raymer doubled up.

"I was particularly proud of that hand. It may not have mattered. He had such a good hand, he might've called my bet anyway. But I really like that hand."

THE RAKE

The important part of this hand is not so much what Raymer had. It is that he had a plan and executed it. Raymer had played with Luske for awhile and had a read on him as a loose-aggressive player, but also as one who can spot a trap. So, Raymer orchestrated a move intended to look orchestrated. Players call it playing one level beyond your opponent.

If Raymer had done the expected—sat back and riffled his chips and thought about it for a while, and then pushed all in—Luske might have folded because he is very good at putting an opponent on a hand.

One-gappers: Cards separated by one rank, i.e., 9-7 and 8-6.
Runner-runner: The last two common cards—fourth street and fifth street—usually used when both cards are needed to make a hand and both cards in fact do come. Also known as running cards.

Raymer's overbet was also a factor. Like most players in that situation, Raymer tended to make a pot-size re-raise. But re-raising all in looked suspicious, giving Luske the impression that Raymer was trying to steal the pot right there.

You don't necessarily need anything as elaborate and audacious as Raymer's act, but you do need to have a plan not limited to one or two hands, but for your entire session. Sure, it will change based on opponents and stack sizes, but being prepared at least for how you plan to start the day—aggressively betting pots or calling to try to outplay the table after the flop, for instance—is crucial to succeeding.

♠ ♦ DAVID "CHIP" REESE ♥ ♣

IN 1974, DAVID "CHIP" REESE WAS IN DAYTON, OHIO, WITH AN ECONOMICS DEGREE from Dartmouth and a job as a manufacturer's representative. Out in Los Angeles was a former girlfriend he was planning to see. And up the coast a bit from her, in Palo Alto, was Stanford University, where his interview for graduate school awaited.

Somewhere in the middle of those three destinations, however, was Las Vegas. And that's as far as Reese got. He has never left. And that's just fine with the man who started in low-limit games before graduating to the biggest games in town to become, at age forty, the youngest person ever inducted into the Poker Hall of Fame.

"I've never been intimidated, and that's one of the things that hurt me and helped me," says Reese, now fifty-four. "When I came out here, the only poker games I'd really played were Seven Card Stud and High-Low Split. They played all different kinds of games here. It was like a track meet. I was never afraid to jump in. I just figured I could jump in and learn. I always had confidence that I could beat them. In retrospect, it was the greatest thing I ever did.

"You have to play all the games. No Limit Hold'em is the popular game because that's what all the tournaments are. But that's not where the money is. We don't even play No Limit Hold'em in a cash game."

Reese, **Doyle Brunson**, Barry Greenstein, Chau Giang, and Phil Ivey—the mainstays of the big game at the Bellagio in Las Vegas—play limit poker. But they play for the highest limits around— say, $4,000-$8,000—and millions are won and lost each year. In addition to Hold'em, they play Seven Card Stud, Omaha 8-or-Better, Pot Limit Hold'em, and Deuce-to-Seven Lowball.

"I know a lot of guys who are good poker players, who've been around a long time, but they were always specialists," Reese says. "They never wanted to venture outside their games. Over the years, sometimes there are some big Seven Card Stud games in town, sometimes there are big Hold'em games, sometimes big Lowball games. Whatever's been popular has always changed. You can survive being a specialist, but you can't play every day. Basically for thirty years, I have walked into the card room, sat down at the biggest game in the world and played whatever they wanted to play. I think a lot of that came from stupidity, really—in my younger years from not being afraid to jump in and play a game I'd never played before and believing I could learn it and beat them."

Reese's impassive, sad-sack poker face at the table belies a sparkling demeanor away from the game, especially when it comes to his family, which includes a twenty-eight-year-old stepdaughter, a fifteen-year-old son, and a twelve-year-old daughter.

"I have a family and kids, and I coach my son in baseball, so when you take that into consideration . . . when he's playing or pitching, if he goes to California to play, I go," Reese says. "There's no poker game that can keep me away from that."

Reese had never been much for tournaments because, well, that is not where the money is for an everyday gambler. "There's a fine line between coming in fiftieth and winning," Reese says. "The flip of a card—A-K versus two jacks. And the amount of time it takes, when you really put a paper and pencil to it, if you're at my level, it's not really worth it. I can go in and play in games every day where $200,000 is just a normal win or loss. You play all the different games, so your skill is really coming into play more than in the tournaments.

"I started playing tournaments lately because my kids want to see me on television. That's the only reason."

And so, the legendary cash game player says the best hand he ever played—"the most memorable"—came when he first hit Vegas in 1974.

"I came to town with $400. I was playing $30-$60 limit, and I had a buddy who came out with me at the time and we put in together. We built our bankroll to about $30,000. I was playing Seven Card Stud and I looked over—it was at the Flamingo Hotel; Johnny Moss had the Flamingo Hotel around 1974—and they were playing a black chip game, $400-$800 high-low split.

"I didn't know any of these people, but it was Doyle Brunson and Johnny Moss and Puggy Pearson and Nick Vachiano. I'm trying to watch. I played a lot of high-low split in college. And they're playing terrible, a bunch of Texans in there.

"High-Low Split is a game where you have to play low hands, and they're raising with two kings. I can't believe what I'm seeing, but the security guard won't let me near the table. I call my buddy and we've got $30,000 to our names, and we've been working for two months trying to build up this money. I tell him about this game and he said, 'What's the buy-in?' I said, 'The buy-in's $20,000, but that's not enough. We're going to have to buy in for all our money.' He said, 'Are you crazy?' I said, 'There's no chance I can lose in this game.' These were the best players in the world.

Black chip game: A table where the lowest denomination of chips is $100, which is the black chip in most casinos. **Wheel:** A straight consisting of A-2-3-4-5; also known as a baby straight. **Loose game:** Many players seeing the flop and playing marginal cards. **Tight game:** Few players seeing the flop and betting only premium hands. **Fish:** Bad players; also known as dead money. **Freerolling:** When you already have the nut low or nut high in a split game, you are getting a free shot to improve your hand enough to also win the other half of the pot.

"Finally, I talked him into getting into the game, and $30,000 isn't very much. I got in the game, I'm winning a little bit and this hand comes up. In the first five cards, I had a 1-2-3-4-6, the second-best low you can have, and I had 1-2-3-4 hearts. Doyle was in the pot, and he had big cards showing. Puggy was in, too. I never raised and they all raised. The only guy that had low cards showing was Nick Vachiano. He had a 6 and a 5 showing with a king, so he couldn't beat me unless he caught two perfect to a wheel.

"They tried to raise me out of the pot because I was a young kid. I just kept calling. The last card, I look down and squeeze the cards and caught a 'two-across' heart, which means it's a 4 or 5 of hearts. If you look on the spots on a card, there are two spots for a

4 or a 5. I already had A-2-3-4 hearts, so I made an ace-flush wheel. I won a profit of about $29,000 in this pot. The pot probably had $60,000, $70,000. It was the most exciting hand for me. By the end of the weekend, I had about $360,000 playing in that High-Low Split game and that's what started it all.

"That hand was very memorable because it was so important and I found out who these guys were. I just started playing and went to the next level. I went from playing in a small game to playing in a real big game and never quit."

THE RAKE

How many times have you walked into a card room, put your name on a list, and tried to kill time until you were called? Well, don't do it again.

Find out which tables are dealing your game and scout the players. Is it a loose game or tight? Are a lot of players seeing the flop? Are they seeing the flop with good hands? Or can you win only with the nuts? Find out which tables are filled with fish and get yourself to one of them. After all, you are there for the cash, right?

That is pretty much what Chip Reese did back in 1974. He was playing in a $30-$60 game that was as big as his bankroll could handle, but then he spotted a bigger game—the biggest—that he believed he could win.

The hand itself is a lesson in nerve—to play the game for such big stakes and to stand up to bigger bankrolls in the face of raises meant to run him out. Reese had a good hand to start with and a great one as it turned out, and yet he never put in for a raise. It is savvy play when you can let someone else bet your hand for you.

The advantage of Reese's pre-scouting was that he determined his opponents would bet big cards in a small-card game. What's more, he knew they would also bet with questionable low hands. Just one opponent appeared to be Reese's competition for the low half of the pot, but only if he caught the right two cards. Reese essentially was freerolling for the high hand. That is the surest route to scooping a pot, which is where you make the big money in High-Low Split games.

♠♦ RON ROSE ♥♣

RON ROSE, THE MAN WHO WROTE THE BOOK ON POKER PLAYERS, is certainly worth a chapter himself. The white-haired, bespectacled Ohioan ran a profitable Internet company that he sold in 1999. Rather than retire at forty-five, Rose turned to bridge, which he hadn't played since high school. No matter. In just a year's time, he became a Life Master and won the Mini-McKinney Award, given to the best player in North America. After that, he set out to conquer poker.

"The first tournament I ever played in was the World Series in 2000," says Rose, author of *Poker Aces—The Stars of Tournament Poker.* "I played with all the biggies. I played in eight one-table satellites and I won five. I thought, This is pretty easy pickings. I spent a small percentage of the amount and I got into each of these events. I cashed in one of the events that year."

Rose then moved on to Europe and in less than a year, he found himself in five events, three in an eight-day period at the Aviation Club in France. He followed that run with a sixth-place finish in the World Poker Finals at Foxwoods Resort Casino and a win in the World Poker Challenge at the Reno Hilton during the World Poker Tour's first season, then captured the WPT Battle of Champions at the Bellagio.

Fittingly, Rose says the best hand he ever played came during the WPT Battle of Champions that aired on Super Bowl Sunday in 2004.

"They had all the champions of the World Poker Tour that year and they played one another. I wanted to win that particular event very much so I could have bragging rights. To me, if I could beat all the champions of the World Poker Tour, it would be quite an accomplishment.

"My most memorable hand was the last one. I was playing against José Rosenkrantz and I had a 2-1 chip lead. I get dealt a 7 and a jack of diamonds. The blinds were probably $20,000-$40,000. I got in for real cheap because the blinds were big. So I just called the $20,000 and limped in."

The flop came J-10-7, giving Rose top and bottom pair. "I love it. I'm thinking, 'Boy, maybe this is the hand that I can trap him with a little bit.' I have two pair off the get-go, and I check it. He looks at his hand and he has K-Q. He has the J-10 on board. So he loves it too.

"He makes a bet and I raise. He pushes all in. He had about $1.6 million in chips left. I had him about 2-1 in chips. I'm saying, 'Oh, my god, I just trapped him good.' But he does have an open-ended straight draw. I call."

The turn came a queen. "Oh, my gosh. What that means is, with my jacks and 7's, if the board pairs the 10, I lose. He gets an ace, a jack, a 10, queen, king, or 9, and guess what? I lose.

"The river card comes the 4 of hearts. The 4 of hearts was, like, my love card because in several previous hands, I had won big pots during the day with it. It was my most satisfying hand for the fact that I accomplished what I set out to do there. My objective was to win the tournament, and I did with that hand."

THE RAKE

When you're playing short-handed, almost anything goes. The range of hands you will play widens considerably. With J-7 suited—meaning he had potential flush and straight draws, not to mention the chance to pair his jack—and with a chip advantage of about $3.2 million to about $1.6 million, there was no doubt Rose would call the big blind for just $20,000 more. But holding K-Q, Rosenkrantz missed a chance for a preflop raise of, say, $150,000 or $200,000 that might have dissuaded Rose from continuing with the hand.

Rosenkrantz was on a semi-bluff. He didn't have the best hand—he was a 2-1 underdog on the flop—but he had the best chance to draw out to the best hand. Rose, of course, was wrong about a jack helping Rosenkrantz, because that would have given Rose jacks full of sevens. But as it was, Rosenkrantz had sixteen cards that would make his hand.

Rosenkrantz, it seemed, was trying to trap Rose by letting him see the flop, but then, once it came, Rose was setting a trap for Rosenkrantz. With top and bottom pair, Rose raised Rosenkrantz to accomplish one of two things: Win the pot right there if Rosenkrantz was on a draw and missed, or get all of Rosenkrantz's money into the middle when he had the best of it.

It is also worth noting Rose's raise on the flop and then his call of Rosenkrantz's all in. Both moves show the power of being the chip leader. First, Rose could use his big stack to put the pressure on Rosenkrantz to call a raise on the flop.

Trap: To feign weakness with a strong hand in hopes of getting your opponent to bet big. **Open-ended straight draw:** To have four consecutive cards and need either a card at either end to complete the straight, i.e., having 4-5-6-7 and needing either an 8 or a 3 to make the hand. **Short-handed:** Playing at a table that is not full.

Then, the power of Rose's money enabled him to treat Rosenkrantz's all in as just another bet, knowing that even if he lost, he would still have plenty of chips to play with. It is a big weapon when an all in can end your opponent's game, but not yours.

♠ ◆ ERIK SEIDEL ♥ ♣

ERIK SEIDEL PLAYED AN IMPORTANT ROLE IN THE LEGENDARY 1998 POKER MOVIE *Rounders,* ut it was not a part he auditioned for, nor was it one he necessarily wanted.

In the film, Matt Damon's character, Mike McDermott, watches a tape of the 1988 World Series of Poker main event. Damon's character, an aspiring player in underground New York, is marveling at the way his idol, Johnny Chan, set up his opponent, getting the kid in the red visor to push all in when Chan already held the nuts on what would be the final hand. That kid in the red visor was Seidel.

"I wasn't prepared for that," Seidel says of the actual showdown with Chan. "I had no idea what I was doing [back then]. I didn't know how to play heads-up. I hadn't played it. It was a little bit of an adjustment. I was totally out of my element."

But since that hand, Seidel has become one of the most respected players and has amassed one of the best records against top players heads-up. "I improved a little bit," Seidel says wryly.

Born in Manhattan, Seidel played backgammon from his teenage years to his mid-twenties, one of the many games junkies who have come to poker. "I knew a couple people who played poker, like **Chip Reese** and Stu Ungar, because they were backgammon players," Seidel says. "They started playing, so I started playing. I was very impressed with both of them. I didn't really have any goal to be in that kind of class. It looked like a fun game and I thought I should try it." Seidel had been trying it only a few years when he made it to that final showdown against Chan at the World Series of Poker.

Despite being humble to the point where he can't figure out why he draws public attention, Seidel has won six World Series of Poker bracelets. He made the final table of the main event in 1999, an accomplishment that was also the site of the best hand he ever played.

"We were playing four-handed. I drew A-Q offsuit. I raised [$60,000] before the flop. In a normal ten-handed game, you could consider throwing it away in certain spots. But in a four-handed game, you're never going to throw it away. You're going to lose your money."

Alan Goehring and Chris Bigler called from the blinds. The flop came 8 of clubs, 6 of hearts, 2 of clubs. Everyone checked. The turn came a jack of hearts. Everyone checked again. The river came a 5 of spades. Goehring bet $150,000, Bigler folded and it was on Seidel.

To back up a bit, Goehring had tortured Seidel for a couple of hours the day before, draining him of roughly $500,000 in several big showdowns. So now Seidel was thinking. And thinking. And staring down Goehring for a good two minutes.

"My whole tournament life was at stake. If I was wrong about that, my tournament was over. It was a huge bet. It was a very dangerous call. I would've looked like a total idiot if I had been wrong."

Seidel would have had only about $40,000 left if he called and was wrong. He went all in. Goehring, it turned out, was trying to make a play with Q-10. Seidel's ace-high was good.

"I was either right or wrong. It wasn't a matter of percentages. I was either a complete donkey or I was right, in which case I was going to be back in the game."

THE RAKE

There's no math formula for what Seidel did. It was all read, and as poker players improve, get more experience, and gain confidence, they rely more on their reads. In this case, Seidel had plenty of time to read Goehring and gather information. The hours they had spent crashing into each other—with Goehring usually getting the best of it—had cost Seidel a lot of money. But he got something out of it: a tell.

Seidel believed Goehring was bluffing because of something he saw. It is also something the guarded Seidel refuses to divulge. "It would be very dangerous for me to say what I saw because somebody might use that against me," Seidel says. "Somebody could say, 'Oh, that's what Erik's looking for,' and they could do it. It could be very costly."

But perhaps the first question should be: How did Seidel get this far with A-Q offsuit in the first place? In a normal ten-handed game, you easily could consider folding because you don't have to play many to survive and gather chips. But in a short-handed game, you have to be more active. The range of hands you would consider playing from the different positions widens quite a bit because the blinds are getting bigger and are coming around more often. This is where the math gets you. In four-handed play, for instance, you will have to post blinds in half the hands each round. If you are on a short stack at the $100-$200 level in a tournament where you start with $1,000 in chips, that's $300 in blinds, which can easily be 25-50 percent of your chips.

So, not only do you need to play more hands but you also need to be able to play better after the flop because you will be in more hands. Part of that post-flop play includes reading an opponent's style and betting patterns the way Seidel read Goehring.

♠♦ MIKE SEXTON ♥♣

MIKE SEXTON IS BEST KNOWN AS THE KNOWLEDGEABLE, ENTHUSIASTIC COHOST OF the World Poker Tour on the Travel Channel, but he has been a professional poker player for more than twenty-five years.

Like many, Sexton started his career while attending colle his main emphasis was maintaining the gymnastics scholarship he earned at Ohio State University in the 1960s. "My best event actually was bouncing on the trampoline," Sexton says. "That was still an event in the NCAA at the time. In fact, my senior year was the last year the trampoline was an event. Then they went to the six Olympic events."

Before pursuing poker full-time, Sexton worked as a sales- man, taught some ballroom dancing, and even served in the mili- tary. "I always wanted to be a paratrooper," he says. "I always wanted to jump out of planes. You've got to remember, I've been doing flips all my life, so the next step for me after I got out of college was to go flip out of a plane. So, that's what I did, jumping 1,500 feet.

"I was in the 82nd Airborne division, and I came very close to making it a career actu- ally. I was very fortunate because they had just come back from Vietnam when I joined the unit. I was stationed in Fort Bragg all my time in the service. When I was young, I said, 'If I've got to go, I've got to go.' Looking back on it now, it was quite a blessing."

These days, Sexton says he could never imagine how profitable pursuing poker full- time would become. "For over twenty years, I didn't have a paycheck," he says. "I'd lit- erally play poker five, six days a week, every week. Then, when I created the Tournament of Champions of Poker, that got me over to the business side a little bit. It was a presti- gious event in poker in 1999, 2000, and 2001. I think it was the most elite event ever in poker. Honestly, it was before its time, before the World Poker Tour came about. I put it on, but we never made money on it, so I had to give it up. That last year, I had the opportunity to go to work for PartyPoker.com. That came probably as a result of putting the Tournament of Champions together, and I became well-known in the poker indus- try. Really, that's where I was very fortunate and made my money."

Sexton's down-home charm, mastery of poker strategy and respect for the heart and smarts it takes to reach the top make him a wonderful spokesman for the game. The man with the quick and easy smile likes to describe No Limit Hold'em as a game that "takes five minutes to learn and a lifetime to master."

In his poker lifetime, Sexton has won a World Series of Poker bracelet and played his way near the top of the WSOP list of most cashes. The Indiana native also conquered

Europe in 2000 when he won two events at the Autumn Tournament of the famed Aviation Club in Paris and also took first place in the Euro Finals of Poker No Limit Hold'em Championship. Three years after that, he copped the Heads-up Euro Finals of Poker No Limit Hold'em title.

Sexton says the best hand he ever played came in the 1989 World Series of Poker in the Seven Card Stud Limit High-Low Split tournament:"At that time, I was playing Seven Card Stud High-Low Split all the time, every day, $75-$150 and $50-$100, and I was playing it for a living. I'd never entered the $10,000 tournament at the time, so to me, this was as important as winning the championship event because that was the game that I played all the time.

"What was ironic about that table was that was the first time I went to the final table at the World Series of Poker as the chip leader. The very first deal at the final table, I was rolled up with three 6's, a powerful hand in Seven Card Stud High-Low Split, and I got beat by a flush and it cut my chips in half.

"So, all of a sudden, from being the big chip leader and looking like I was going to walk away with this tournament, I was even with everybody else after one hand, and I thought, 'Oh, no, is this going to happen to me again here?'"

In this hand, the limits were $3,000-$6,000 with a $500 ante. The four remaining players all had about $50,000 in chips. "What happened was, I had to bring it in. I had a 3 up, and the low card brings it in. It went raise, raise, raise, so I threw my hand in. I had 3-7-10 or something like that, and I watched these three other people go to war.

"One guy was rolled up with three kings, one guy was rolled up with three queens, another guy had two aces, and I was the fourth player. I didn't even play this pot. All three went to war with this hand, and one guy broke out the other two players.

"The one player who got busted out with the three queens was **Men "The Master" Nguyen**, one of the great players of all time. I had just met Men. He was just coming into tournament poker at the time. He had the three queens rolled up. Ironically, he never took a raise in this entire hand. The other players took every raise, and he was rolled up with three queens and lost to three rolled-up kings. The other person had aces up and a wheel draw, so all three had really powerful hands.

Seven Card Stud Limit High-Low Split: A Seven Card Stud game with preset betting limits where the best high hand splits the pot with the best low hand. **Bring it in:** A forced first bet; in high-low split games, it is the lowest card that makes the first bet; in high-only games, it is the highest card that leads the betting. **Rolled up:** When your first three cards match in Seven Card Stud, i.e., when your two hole cards are 6's and your first exposed card is also a 6. **Aces up:** A hand with two pair, one of which is aces. **Cold call:** A player who matches an opponent's raise.

"Ironically, my greatest hand wasn't a hand I was even involved in, but it put me in a position to win the tournament, and that's what happened. When I got heads-up, the other player had a 3-1 chip advantage on me, but it vaulted me up $70,000 in real money with a chance to win this tournament.

"That took a series of hands before I could come back and beat this guy. But I wasn't in any hurry, of course. I just methodically built my chips up and just caught better cards than him in the heads-up battle and it went my way.

"That was my first bracelet. That's why it was so exciting. I wanted one so bad. You have to remember, I'd been a professional player for, like, ten or twelve years and I'd only been to the World Series four or five years, but to me at that time, winning a bracelet identified you as having achieved something."

THE RAKE

It's a pretty simple concept, but it can't be said enough: Folding is a regular part of your poker arsenal. It has to be. The best players say they muck their starting hands about 80 percent of the time. Sure, it was easy for Sexton to lay down 10-7-3 behind a couple of raises and a cold call because 10-7-3 offsuit does not play well in many poker games.

But this hand also presents a strategic situation that is less about playing a specific hand than it is about sitting down at a table with a plan to win, whether it is at a final table that you are good enough to make or even a single-table satellite that you enter. When every other player at the table is going to war, you have a chance to move up the chip ladder because one player—or in Sexton's case, two—will lose a chunk of chips, if not all of them. Any time you can let opponents wipe each other out, you gain, both in chip status and real money paid out for the descending places of finish. Sure, the player who won the hand that Sexton cited had him out-chipped 3-1 when they got to heads-up play, but suddenly there were two fewer opponents that Sexton had to get past—in hard cash, that meant $70,000—and Sexton was able to come back and win the event.

♠♦ CHARLIE SHOTEN ♥♣

CHARLIE SHOTEN HAS BEEN PLAYING CARDS FOR MOST OF HIS sixty-eight years. He can trace it back to being five years old and coming from a home where the poker table took the place of the dinner table. "The only place my family—my uncles and my aunts—really talked and got together was around the poker table," he recalls. "Poker became a stay of my life."

Eventually, the New York-born Shoten, who graduated from the University of Alabama, developed a computer software company in the '60s. But technology changes cost him his business in 1985. Those pressures, compounded by being a single parent, landed Shoten in the hospital.

"I lost everything," he says. "I was playing at two craps tables at the same time in Atlantic City. I had five years in recovery and I had a five-year pin from Gamblers Anonymous."

And yet, Shoten (who at one point was so worried that people would find out how much money he was winning that he adopted the moniker Scotty Warbucks—no doubt because of his resemblance to Little Orphan Annie's Daddy Warbucks) could not give up poker. But he was not winning much because of tendencies he described as "self-destructive." Moving to Southern California, Shoten says he began to change his thinking in 2001 and developed a new attitude that he has detailed in a book called *Play Winning No Limit Hold'em and Life.*

"The main part of the book is 'and Life,'" he says. "What I talk about is how in the last three years I developed my own road map for becoming a happier person and really letting go of a lot of the distractions."

Shoten's method might not be for everybody, but it has certainly worked for him. In 2003, he reached nineteen final tables of major tournaments and earned a top ten ranking in the Player of the Year standings. He took second in both the California State Poker No Limit Hold'em Championship and the World Poker Tour's Poker Open. In 2004, he came sixth in the World Series of Poker's Seven Card Stud championship.

Shoten says the best hand he ever played—or at least the most unusual—came in a cash game at the Commerce Casino. "I was playing in a $100-$200 Limit Hold'em game. I was dealt A-K offsuit. There were about five, six people in the pot. It was capped, which means it was raised to the limit with about five or six people. There was about $2,500 in the pot pre-flop."

The flop came A-8-8. Again, the pot was capped, making it worth about $5,000. "The turn card came an ace. It was also capped on the turn with about three people in the pot because I had aces full and the other person had four eights [meaning the pot was about $7,500]. And the river was an ace. My opponent flopped four 8's. I flopped a pair of aces and I bought two more aces on the turn and the river.

"The other person made a crying call when they saw the third ace come out. They knew they were beat, but they had to call. How often does it happen that you get a thousand-to-one shot in a big game on that kind of a flop?"

THE RAKE

At first glance, this looks like an instance of betting a hand to the river based on implied pot odds. In fact, this is just a case where Shoten got lucky because he was indeed a virtual 1,000-1 shot to hit the runner-runner aces he needed to beat his opponent.

Poker players tend to look for any reason to call a bet, especially when the pot gets big. They rationalize their play based on the concepts of pot odds and implied pot odds, a defense that tends to be as loose as their bets.

Pot odds and implied pot odds are the hardest math lessons in poker. The best players not only understand the concepts, they also apply them correctly. With pot odds, you divide the amount in the pot by the cost of your bet. A simple example: You have to call $10 into a $40 pot, so you are getting 4-1 odds on your money. That means you can miss your card(s) four times, but you can make your hand every fifth time to come

Crying call: Matching your opponent's last bet, even though you believe you are beaten.

out even in the long run. The tricky part is understanding that you are dealing with five total chances—the four $10 bets that are already in the pot, plus your own $10 bet. That bet worth 20 percent of the pot means you need to have at least a 20 percent chance of making your hand. In order to determine whether you have at least a 20 percent chance of doing that, you count the number of unseen cards that can help you. These are called outs.

For instance, if you are holding 7-8 offsuit and the flop comes K-5-6 rainbow, you have an open-ended straight draw. There are four 4's and four 9's that can make your straight, meaning you have eight outs. A quick way to get an approximate calculation of your chances of making your straight with two cards to come is to multiply by four. In this case, eight outs times four equals thirty-two, meaning you have a 32 percent chance to make your hand. Since your bet in the above example is costing you only 20 percent, you are getting good odds to call.

Now then, if pot odds tell you what your bet is worth based on the actual pot, then implied odds tell you what your bet is worth based on the expected pot. In other words, it is how much money you expect to make, knowing that you will win more bets on later streets.

For instance, you might be playing against a serial raiser, so you can calculate how much he'll raise down to the river even if you're only calling. The same goes for a pot similar to Shoten's, where everyone was raising enough to cap each street. By the time Shoten faced a decision on the turn, he figured he could also count on at least the player who was raising with quad 8's to add more money to the pot on the river.

But understand this: Even when you factor in implied odds, the number might not make your call a smart one. Shoten's total call of $800 on the turn into a pot that would be worth about $8,800 gave him 11-1 odds. However, his chances of hitting the case ace were 45-1 (one ace of the remaining forty-six unseen cards). Shoten was getting terrible odds. If he knew his opponent had four 8's, even the extra bets on the river that he could gain would not justify a call and Shoten should have folded.

So why did he play? Because the pot was huge and Shoten had reason to believe he held the best hand. Eventually, against odds of about 1,000-1, he did. Bottom line: If you are going to get lucky, get lucky in a monster pot.

♠♦ BARRY SHULMAN ♥♣

HERE WAS BARRY SHULMAN'S PLAN: RETIRE FROM THE SEATTLE REAL ESTATE business in the mid 1990s, move to Las Vegas, play some golf, a little poker, and stay warm and dry. It sounded simple enough, but there was just one problem. "I wasn't really ready to retire," Shulman says. "So I was just focusing on poker. I was very intellectually interested in the game, found it fascinating, and then I found *Card Player* magazine fascinating because it was—as it is now—pretty much the bible of the industry. I just read it voraciously and I just needed to have my mind doing stuff." So Shulman did what any reasonable, poker-obsessed multimillionaire would do: He walked into the offices of *Card Player* in 1998 and bought it.

"It wasn't even for sale," Shulman says. "I didn't even know the owners. Certainly I knew nothing about journalism or anything like that, but it was clear to me that poker was going to boom and it was clear to me there was a huge upside when I bought it."

Shulman was certainly right about poker booming, as the growing number of television shows, card rooms, Internet sites, magazines, and, yes, poker books will attest. "Many people have said, 'You were in the right place at the right time,'" he says. "Certainly that's true, but I predicted that would happen."

The growth of *Card Player* has also been a family affair. While Shulman holds the title of chairman and publisher and spends much of his time improving the cardplayer.com website, his son, Jeff, serves as chief executive officer and president of the magazine, and Shulman's wife, Allyn, is a staff writer who pens many of the magazine's cover stories.

"We used to have 3,000 people get our newsletter every month, and in two years, we now we have 123,000 every month," Shulman says plainly. "I have no artistic bone in my body. I have no journalistic background, so it's just a function of hiring people who are better than I am who are capable of doing that."

Shulman certainly knows his poker, though. He tends to call himself a businessman who plays poker, but he has solid credentials as a player himself. He won the Seven Card Stud High-Low bracelet event at the World Series of Poker in 2001, the same year he won the Four Queens Poker Classic No Limit Hold'em Championship. In 2002, he finished second in overall best performance in the L.A. Poker Classic. The following year, Shulman came in first in a Five Diamond World Poker Classic No Limit Hold'em tournament and made the final table of the World Poker Tour's Ultimate Bet event.

Shulman says the best hand he ever played was actually a series of hands at the Rio Carnivale of Poker Limit Hold'em tournament in 1998.

"With less than 20 percent of the field left, I was chip leader and feeling pretty good about things and actually beginning to think that perhaps I could win a major event, let alone finish in the money. On the other hand, although trying to focus, my mind was drifting and I was wondering if when the field became short, I would make a fool of myself against the 'name' players.

"Then I was moved to a different table and something amazing happened. Somebody commented on my stack size and how they would all have to give me slack. I didn't say a word because I was really trying my best to focus. I remember picking up two hands in a row, raising both times, picking up the blinds, which by now were quite high, and listening to the others at the table saying how they couldn't stop my bullying. So I didn't let them down.

"I folded hand three, analyzed the situation, said to myself I need another good hand so I can raise because they seem to be playing passively. In retrospect, this seems so very obvious, but it occurred to me I could have garbage and it didn't matter, if they folded. I decided to raise hand four no matter what, even though I was now out of position and fighting every instinct to try to play tight.

"I raised with something random—a non-face-card hand, like a 9-5—and got two calls. Trouble. Nobody re-raised. They must have had high cards but not great. The flop came all low cards, but missed me. I bet. They folded. I never looked back.

"I just started raising every hand and every flop when there was one. The others absolutely declared out loud that they were not going to play with me and would wait for the table to break, which was coming shortly. We played for about twenty minutes. I greatly increased my stack and went on to win the tournament, the first major event I ever won.

"It was the best series of hands I ever played because at that point I knew I could play with anybody. Players often speak of the luck factor in poker. I don't know how to quantify it, but I certainly know that on that day in January 1998, I was not only lucky—there was almost a group self-fulfilling prophecy of my taking all of their chips. But also I finally had the confidence to take advantage of the situation."

THE RAKE

Ah, the power of money. It drives people to poker. It drives people out of tournaments. So playing the bully stack is one of the best lessons you can learn, and Barry Shulman put on a clinic, even if he didn't know he could.

When you have the biggest stack at the table—especially when you have the biggest stack by a lot and when your opponents are commenting on how scared they are of you—then you have the power to control that table. You can raise with nothing and take down pots. You can raise with nothing when you're *out of position* and take down pots.

By betting out from any position, or by raising anyone who bets out, this kind of power poker puts pressure on your opponents. You are constantly testing them, even daring them to call you, and you are letting them know that they will face a decision every time they enter a pot, perhaps a decision for their tournament lives.

It is rare that you will find yourself in such a situation, which is why it is imperative that you command an aggressive table image. More often, you will find yourself at a table with stacks of varying size. The idea then is to determine which of the small stacks are easiest to pick off and maneuver ways to isolate yourself in hands against them. Pay particular attention to the player to your immediate right and the two spots to your immediate left, and here's why: The player to your immediate right always has to make his intentions known before you act, so you are in a position to control him. You are in position to move him off a hand. The importance of the two players to your left comes into play because they will be in the cutoff and on the button when you are also in late position and they will be the blinds when you are on the button. In the case of the former, you have to determine how vigorously they will defend their prized late position advantage in the face of aggressive play; in the latter, you have to determine how willing they are to defend their blinds when you raise.

♠♦ GABRIEL THALER ♥♣

WHEN GABRIEL THALER WAS GROWING UP IN NORTHERN CALIFORNIA, he always knew he would make it to the World Series. He just never imagined it would be the World Series of Poker. But injuries in high school ended Thaler's career as a catcher, so he went to Foothill Junior College to study philosophy, wait tables, and prepare for a teaching degree and a job coaching baseball.

And then he walked into a poker room in California.

"Some members of my family had played a bit of Limit Hold'em," Thaler says, "and I talked to them about it and walked in and started playing $2-$4, $3-$6. I started making more money than I was waiting tables, quit my waiting job, school, and made more money playing poker than I would my first three or four years out of college.

"I realized that five years down the road I would make the same money as a teacher and baseball coach, and I was only playing smaller levels. So, being a single man with not many responsibilities, I quit school and decided to play poker."

In 2000, the then thirty-one-year-old Thaler stepped up from Limit Hold'em to No Limit. At the time, the game's popularity certainly wasn't what it is today. In fact, it was dying on the West Coast, where Thaler lived. But the World Poker Tour came along on the Travel Channel a couple of years later, and everything changed.

"I'm probably the luckiest guy there is because with the TV boom, everybody wants to play No Limit Hold'em," Thaler says. "The second most important thing that happened to me was I essentially gained a mentor once I moved to Los Angeles to play No Limit Hold'em full time: **Bobby Hoff**. He has been a poker professional, a No Limit Hold'em specialist, for forty years.

"I really escalated my game [with Hoff]. He could see in me right away that I had the creativity and the discipline and all the things needed to become a world-class player. For the first two years when I decided to specialize in that game, I just worked hours and hours and hours every day so I could put myself in these situations over again and hone my instincts."

Thaler began concentrating on tournaments in 2003 when the growing number of entrants started making them more lucrative than cash games. It paid off. He finished third in the $3,000 buy-in Pot Limit Hold'em bracelet event at the World Series of Poker, and finished fourth in a $5,000 buy-in No Limit Hold'em event at the Bellagio. Thaler says the best hand he ever played came during a No Limit Hold'em cash game at the Commerce Casino.

"I've played a million hands, but this is definitely the one that explains the finer points of No Limit Hold'em. It's a hand that does not go past the flop, but it's very unique.

"I had a 5-8 unsuited. I was in middle position, about two off the button. No one had entered the pot before my action. I opened the pot for my standard pre-flop raise of $200. Raising with a subpar hand is something I do when I enter a game or shortly after entering a game to sometimes create a false image that I might play more hands than I do in order to get action later in that session. I had only been dealt two or three hands when I raised.

"I was called by a player who had position on me, Huck Seed. The big blind, Prahlad Friedman, who is a very good, very solid, No Limit Hold'em player and has had a lot of success on the Internet, called my raise, so the three of us saw the flop."

The flop came J-3-4, rainbow. "Prahlad, who was first to act, led out into me, the pre-flop raiser, about $500—or about 80 percent of the pot. I decided that knowing Prahlad very well and knowing the history he and I have—we both respect each other's play—that he was kind of testing me. I also know that he is very capable of leading out into a flop of J-3-4 where there are not many draws apparent with no hand at all. If there are only two or three players in this pot, it's very likely that none of them are paired at this point if they did not start out paired. And if they were paired lower than a jack, it's very likely they'd throw their hand away."

Thaler thought that if he raised, Friedman would believe he had a hand that could beat jacks and would not want to call not only the raise but also two more bets on the turn and the river if he held only one pair.

Middle position: Generally referring to seats 4, 5, and 6 in the betting order of a particular round.
Lead out: To open the betting; to lead out into the original bettor or the raiser as a way of pressuring the opponent and representing strength.

"So I stated 'raise' verbally to the dealer and threw out the amount that equaled his bet so I could be certain of the amount of the pot and finish my raise. At the time when I threw out my call, Huck Seed, the player behind me, did not hear that I said 'Raise,' and threw out a stack of $100 bills—approximately $2,500, which was everything he had in front of him. The dealer says, 'Whoa, whoa, whoa, it's not your turn yet.' Huck says, 'Oh, I'm sorry. I didn't hear him raise.'

"So now I'm in kind of a quandary. I have an 8 and a 5. The board is J-3-4, and I know that Huck Seed wants to play his hand at this point. But I'm also verbally committed to raising. I must raise now. So, I tried to decide the best course of action.

"Do I just want to raise the minimum—another $500—and give up on my hand, assuming that he is going to play his hand no matter what? Or do I want to make a very large raise to try to intimidate him out of the pot?

"After some short deliberation, I decided to raise $1,200, which was approximately 75 percent of the pot.

"I also had quite a bit of history with Huck Seed. He respects me as a solid player. I was trying to confuse him as to whether he thought I was trying to bring him in the pot or scare him out of the pot with my bet. Because now I have information. I know what his action was going to be. I know he wants to play his hand. Am I trying to get him to play his hand or am I trying to get him to throw his hand away?

"Huck went through some deliberation and he said, 'I fold,' while still retaining his cards. It did not necessarily follow the rules, but I definitely wasn't going to be bothered. I know he wasn't going to try to take an angle. The other player in the pot didn't seem to be bothered.

"Now it goes back to Prahlad, and after some deliberation he looks me over, gives me the study, and shows a king and a jack, and folds. At that time, Huck Seed exposes his hand, which is two queens, and says, 'I had that hand beat,' and then throws his hand in the muck.

"And I rake in this pot in which I made two players throw away far superior hands. I threw my hand in facedown and neither of them ever knew. They may have said something about my hand, but I didn't reply. My goal is not to embarrass anyone. My goal is just to win the money."

THE RAKE

This hand illustrates the importance of knowing your opponents and the many levels of thinking sometimes required in No Limit Hold'em, where you need to be able to force opponents to throw away better hands, even when you know an opponent desperately wants to play his hand.

In Thaler's case, he had logged hours against Seed and Friedman, so he knew what kind of players they were and he knew what kind of player they thought he was. Thaler knew Friedman was testing him by betting out into him on the flop, but Thaler also knew Friedman likely didn't hold a hand that could take much heat, which is why he re-raised.

But before he could announce the amount of his raise, Thaler got some information from Seed's throwing all those Benjamins into the pot. The key, then, was the amount of Thaler's raise—$1,200. It represented 75 percent of the pot, within the range that Thaler normally raises when he has a hand. If he had gone all in, it would've looked like a suspicious scare tactic. If he raised just half the pot, it would've looked like what it was—a stone bluff that was designed to display weakness but would be transparent to a seasoned player such as Seed. And indeed, because Thaler bet far more than the minimum $500, Seed read the raise as someone not crazy enough to throw big money into a player who had a hand he obviously wanted to play.

The mistake most inexperienced players make when betting is that they shove out the same amount on the river as they did on the turn. For example, a $1,200 bet on fourth street into a $1,600 pot shows strength. But betting the same $1,200 on the river into what is now a $4,000 pot is less than 33 percent and screams weakness. The better players look at that as a bet that represents the amount you're willing to lose, not the amount that it takes to win the pot. If the river doesn't help the inexperienced player, he finds himself not wanting to check to show weakness, but a bet that is only one-third of the pot is the same as showing weakness. If you're going to bet, bet like you mean it.

♠♦ DEWEY TOMKO ♥♣

TALK TO DEWEY TOMKO'S FRIENDS, AND THEY WILL TELL YOU THAT HE IS JUST A BIG kid at heart. So it was only natural that he would become a kindergarten teacher. The problem was, while he was teaching in Florida there was just too much money to be made in poker games. And operating a casino. And owning a golf course. And just about any other business the Runyonesque Pennsylvania native would eventually get into.

"I grew up in a pool hall, playing poker in the backroom when I was fifteen, sixteen," he recalls. "I worked my way through school playing poker with all the GIs coming home from the Vietnam War. We all played poker and I made enough money to get through school. When I got out of college, I continued to play.

"I eventually had to quit teaching kindergarten. I loved it, but at $6,100 a year, I just couldn't make enough money. I'd be leaving a poker game at seven o'clock in the morning to go teach school for $35 a day. That's how I got out of it. It cost me too much money to teach."

Tomko began venturing outside Florida and was on his way to a worldwide reputation, highlighted by twice coming *thisclose* to winning the World Series of Poker main event. Sadly for Tomko, he lost both times when his opponents—Jack Straus in 1982, Carlos Mortensen in 2001—sucked out on the river.

"There are certain kinds of luck and destiny involved," the fifty-nine-year-old Tomko says. "I had the best hand both times until the last card and I lost them both. I have no regrets, though. They used to say there was a hex in the old days—that all the guys who used to win would go broke the next year. Luckily enough, I didn't win it, so I didn't go broke. Maybe it kept me focused on trying to be a better player and making more money."

Tomko finished second in about fifteen events in the 1980s, and then won almost every tournament worth winning, from three World Series of Poker bracelets to the Irish Eccentric to the Grand Prix of Poker back-to-back, and was regarded for a time as the best tournament player in the world.

"After I won those two back-to-back, it was like when I talked to Lawrence Taylor and he said after he won the first Super Bowl, it was such a letdown," Tomko explains. "He reached his goal. I reached my goal to win these tournaments and become the best player, and I thought there'd be this great feeling and it wasn't there.

"I used to play poker three days in a row, sleep a day, play for fifteen years, and I'd wake up and didn't know who the president of the United States was. That's all I did. The

Grand Prix was as big as the World Series in those days. I thought there'd be this big thing because I finally reached it—and there was nothing there.

"From there on in, I had three boys growing up—they were nine, five, and two at the time—and I just went home and went to every practice, every baseball game for fifteen years as they all grew up. Once they were all grown up, I started getting back in poker about 2001."

True story about one of those grown-up sons, Derek: Tomko wanted to name his first son Takhomasak because that's the neon sign over the cash register at the Steak 'n' Shake restaurants where Tomko used to eat just about every day. Tomko's wife stepped in and said no way. "I was going to call him Taki, " Tomko says pleadingly.

That episode provides just a peek into why some people consider Tomko such a character, and fitting his history, Tomko says the best hand he ever played came in a No Limit Hold'em cash game at the Golden Nugget in the 1970s against one of the most feared men in Texas and Las Vegas and all points in between.

"The guy's name is R.D. Matthews. He's still living. You ask a Texan about R.D. Matthews, and they'll start shakin' on the phone because he was the meanest, roughest guy ever in Texas. He was Benny Binion's bodyguard, did all the dirty work.

"This guy used to hang around the Horseshoe when I was young. This was back in '74, when Derek was born. That's one of the reasons I had to play this hand the way it was, because I had a young kid.

Suck out: To have the worst hand heading into the river, but drawing a card that makes your hand a winner. **Case:** The last of anything. In a deck, if there are three aces out and you draw the fourth, you've drawn the case ace.

"R.D. was a big man and he had a black patch over his eye. Toughest *sumbitch* in the world. You beep the horn at him and he'd get out a baseball bat and just break every window in your car. One of those kind of guys. He walked around the casino and everybody was petrified of him.

"He used to play a little poker. When he used to go drinking and get drunk, everybody knew to stay out of his way. He was a mean drunk.

"There are stories about him playing poker and telling somebody, 'If you don't lose this hand to me, I'm going to kill the next person who beats me,' and they'd throw their hand away.

"So, we're at the Golden Nugget card room years ago, and it's a real cheap game, like a $1-$2-$5 No Limit. That's all I can afford in those days because I'm making $6,100 a year teaching kindergarten. I've got a $10,000 bankroll to my name and I'm out there in the summer between school years. I'm out there trying to make a living and I'm stuck in this poker game. R.D.'s playing in this poker game and he's terrorizing everybody. And he's drunk.

"Well, I'm about a $5,000 loser. I don't know what to do. It's my whole bankroll. I've got kids, everything like that, and R.D. and I get tied up in this pot. I've got about $5,000 lost and I've got my last $5,000 on the table. I have to figure out how to get my $5,000 back. And if I lose this, I don't know what I'm going to do. I can't even get back to Florida.

"He's got J-J, but nobody knows what he's got in the beginning. I raise it up before the flop. R.D. calls. It's just him and me on this flop, and he starts telling everybody, 'I'm going to kill the next person who tries to bluff me out of a pot.' But I have to get my money back.

"The flop comes something like 10-5-2. He bets a little bit and I raise him. I'm on a bluff, but he doesn't know this. He's sitting there studying and studying, drinking whiskey, showing everybody he's got a gun. He gives me a lecture. He says, 'Son, you better not be stealing from me, because if you're stealing from me, I'm going to god-damn kill your ass.'

"Finally, he decides to call. I might've bet him $100 at the start, but now there's money in the pot because we're playing No Limit.

"Next card comes off a blank. He checks. I bet him about $1,300. It doesn't seem like a lot, but it's a lot for me because I'm on my case money in those days. He studies and studies and studies, and he gives another lecture about how he's going to kill anybody that's bluffing at him.

"I don't know what the hell to do, because I can't leave my money out there because I ain't got anymore, so I'm sweating, everybody's looking at me. They don't even like the idea of my betting because he didn't even want anybody to bet him; he just wanted everybody to give him the pot.

"But I ain't got no choice. I got all my money out there and I ain't got no more. So I bet him again on fourth street. He studies and studies and studies and gives me a lec-ture about how he's in a mood to kill somebody and how 'I ain't put nobody in the desert in a long time,' and the problem is, he could do it.

"Anyhow, he says, 'I'm going to call your little stinkin' ass,' and he said, 'You better not be bluffing.' So now I've got nothing. All the money's out there, about $4,000, and I've got about $3,000 left.

"The next card comes a blank. He checks again. Now, I can't just give this pot up because my money's in there, you understand? So I moved all in on him. I bet my last $3,000, and, buddy, it's the longest five or ten minutes of my life. He sat there and studied and he studied and he studied, and told me if I was bluffing at this pot, he's going to kill me. I can't say nothing, you know what I mean?

"He says, 'I'll tell you one thing, son. You better not be bluffing. I still might call you, but if I don't call you, you better show me this goddamn hand to see if you ain't bluffing because I'm going to kill you if you are.'

"So I'm sitting there sweating. I have no idea what I'm doing. It's my case money, so I can't check it. I've got to bet it.And I'm thinking, 'What the hell am I going to do?' If he calls me and wins, it's going to be okay because he's at least going to win the pot. But if he doesn't call me and wants to see my hand, what am I going to do?

"Anyway, he says, 'I ain't calling. I'm out. But I want to see that hand.' Here's what I did: I grabbed my hand and threw it into the muck real quick. He started steamin' because I didn't show him the hand. So I said, 'R.D., I had two kings. I knew I had you. I ain't allowed to show my hand; it's against the rules to show it, but I had two kings and I had you. I knew you didn't have that beat, or you would've called. Believe me, I had two kings. You made the right decision. You know I'd never bluff you in a situation like that.'

"I still have nightmares about that hand. If the dealer had ever turned it up after I threw it into the middle of the muck, I might not be living. I got my money back and headed right back to Florida before I got killed. I was losing and I had to get my money back. I couldn't just sit there and give up every pot to him. I was young and stupid."

THE RAKE

You know, for all the poker you see on TV and all that is written and discussed regarding the game, you just don't get enough how-to advice on handling liquored-up, gun-waving, life-threatening players with nefarious backgrounds.

To think, all of Dewey Tomko's sweating and R.D. Matthews' menacing came simply because Tomko was trying to steal the blinds and antes with a pre-flop raise.

Tomko re-raised after the flop to take another shot at stealing the pot, but Matthews called (and let Tomko know exactly what he thought of bluffers). Tomko bet again on the turn, and when he was called for the third straight time, he knew he was up against a premium hand. He also knew he had a chance to get away from the hand. But he chose to sell the bluff as big as he could, which meant going all in on the river.

The fact that his opponent was checking and calling led Tomko to believe he wasn't up against aces, and probably not kings, either. As his stack was dwindling, especially on fourth street, Tomko was in danger of being trapped in a re-raise all in by Matthews because Tomko was pot-committed. But when Matthews merely called, Tomko could carry on his bluff by representing a bigger hand. Or at least by telling the dangerous Matthews that he had a bigger hand.

And it worked. Some quick thinking and sharp talking by Tomko let him win the pot and live to tell the story thirty years later. You have to play the hand the way the hand has to be played in all circumstances. If you have to bluff to win it, you have to bluff to win it.

Even if your life is at stake.

♠ ♦ DAVID "DEVILFISH" ULLIOTT ♥ ♣

LET'S START WITH THAT NICKNAME. "A GUY CALLED STEVIE YOUNG GAVE ME THE NAME," Devilfish says in that Yorkshire accent that brings him back to his home of Hull, England. "He said, 'You're a devilfish.' It's a fish where if they don't take the poison out, people get killed when they eat it.

"In January 1997, I had just come to Vegas for the first time. I was playing Men the Monkey, as I call **Men the Master**. We were heads-up in the Omaha tournament, and somebody shouted 'Go on, The Master.' Gary Whitacre, my driver, immediately shouted out, 'Go on, Devilfish,' and the headlines the next day were 'The Devilfish devours The Master.' I came back in April for the World Series and put Devilfish on the bracelet for a bit of fun."

Ah, yes. The World Series of Poker bracelet. Ulliott won it in the Pot Limit Hold'em event in 1997. Finally, he had found a place that would let him ante up. Early on, you see, Ulliott couldn't get a game. No one would play with him. The "Devilguppy," as it were, was too good. Friends back home would move games without telling him. Other players simply wouldn't show up for home games where he had been invited. Even family members ran him off.

"I was playing Five Card Stud, poker like in *The Cincinnati Kid* in England, and it got to the point where I couldn't get any more games in my local area because I was too good for them," Ulliott says. "I moved to London and other places and started learning new games—Omaha, Texas Hold'em, Seven Card Stud.

"I've been a hustler all my life. I used to play pool, snooker, bet the horses. I've been playing poker for nearly thirty years. Money doesn't frighten me. A lot of people are afraid to put the money in the pot. When you're playing heads-up you have to be fearless.

"Going back to 1997, the same year, I played **Lyle Berman** heads-up and took $168,000 in a cash game. I've played lots of head-up matches since and have a good record."

The fact is Ulliott has a good record, period. In 2004, he won the British Open No Limit Hold'em Championship and the World Heads-Up Poker Championship Pot Limit Omaha event. The year before, he won the World Poker Tour's World Poker Open No Limit Hold'em Championship, and the year before that, he won the World Poker Open Pot Limit Omaha title. Twice he has finished second in World Series of Poker events.

As if Ulliott's game weren't flashy enough, his sense of style is all in. He is usually found wearing an immaculately cut suit and tie, slicked-back dark hair, orange-tinted prescription glasses and a ring on each hand that is so huge it requires two fingers to display. Naturally, one ring says Devil, the other Fish.

"It's nice to look nice," Ulliott says. "Women like to see guys in a suit. Women don't like to see guys playing at the final table in vests and caps and T-shirts and scruffy jeans. Poker's got a bit of class to it, you know. And we want to make people know that. It's not the backroom poker it used to be. I mean, I used to play at places where they had a pig's head on the wall for an air freshener and the sawdust on the floor was last night's furniture."

Five Card Stud: A game in which each player gets one card down and four cards up with betting after each exposed card.

Ulliott says the best hand he ever played—"certainly this is the most unusual"—came during the Pot Limit Hold'em championship in the World Series of Poker in 1997:"I'd just got heads-up with a guy named Chris Trilby from England. We're both about the same chips and this hand came down, which is quite amazing for Texas Hold'em."

Ulliott drew A-4 of hearts. Trilby held 7-7. The flop came 7-5-3 with two hearts. "Chris has flopped top set and I have the one hand which is nearly even money against him—the A-4 of hearts, which means I could win with a deuce to get the wheel or I could win with the 6 to get the 7-high straight, or a heart for the flush draw. He was a slight favorite, but it was close to even money.

"I bet, he raised, and I re-raised. I'm trying to win the hand right there and then. All the money went in on the flop. I was happy to put it all in there. I missed it on the turn, but the last card came off a deuce. And that's how I won my first World Series bracelet.

"That was very unusual to have it happen like that, when a guy flops top set and he can't believe it when he's getting action, and unbeknownst to him, he's barely even money. In Omaha, it's a hand that happens all the time. In Hold'em, it's very difficult for this to come down where you've got a straight draw and the nut flush draw.

"It was nice when the deuce turned. I had about five friends in the audience who were screaming, 'Six, deuce, heart, six, deuce, heart,' and the deuce came up and there was a massive cheer."

THE RAKE

The last thing you want to do with a big draw is actually have to draw to it, even if you have a flush draw and a straight draw the way Ulliott did. That's why Ulliott raised pre-flop and that's why he not only bet out but also re-raised after the flop.

At that point, Ulliott was counting any ace as another likely out, but since he did not have a made hand, he was trying to win the pot right there, hoping his aggressive betting would run off an opponent who might be holding only one 7. But Trilby had a set. He wasn't going anywhere, except all in.

Pre-flop, Ulliott's A-4 of hearts against Trilby's wired 7's made him an underdog by almost 2-1. After the 7-5-3 flop with two hearts, Ulliott didn't hold quite the even-money hand he thought, rating as only 40 percent to win.

But when all the money got in on the flop, his semi-bluff left him with what appeared to be seventeen outs to catch twice. He had a shot at any of the nine hearts to make his flush, or any of the four deuces or the four 6's to make his straight, and he needed only one of them to come up on either the turn or the river.

The potential problem was that Ulliott's outs were reduced to fifteen because if fourth street and fifth street came running deuces or running 6's, Trilby made a full house with 7's over. This point is an easily overlooked part of figuring pot odds and outs: A card that might help you make your hand might also give your opponent the nuts.

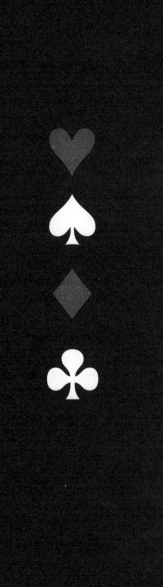

♠ ◆ AMIR VAHEDI ♥ ♣

HE IS KNOWN FOR BRANDISHING AN UNLIT CIGAR AT THE BATTLEGROUND THAT IS THE
poker table, but not so long ago Amir Vahedi was brandishing something far more
dangerous on an actual battleground: a rifle in the Iran-Iraq war in the 1980s.

Vahedi fought to defend his native Iran for nineteen months, including three and
a half months on the front lines. After a short leave at home, with his mother crying
and begging him not to return, Vahedi sneaked out of the country and into Pakistan.
Freedom was short-lived, however, as he was arrested in Afghanistan for lack of doc-
umentation and jailed for ten months. Upon his release, Vahedi "traveled the world
with a phony passport until I settled in the United States as a refugee" in 1983.

Once in the States, Vahedi managed a backgammon club in Beverly Hills and
caught a whiff of casino action while serving as a driver for an old Iranian general who
liked to play poker at a club in Gardena, California. Bored, Vahedi
played some 50-cent/$1 poker, but didn't take it seriously. "I was a
big fish," said Vahedi, preferring the more conventional games a
casino offered.

By 1997, Vahedi decided he would either make a living at
gambling or not play at all. He happened to enter a $10 tourna-
ment with re-buys, and turned a $60 investment into a $1,300
payday by winning the event. That's when Vahedi knew he had
the talent for tournament poker.

A soft-spoken man who can easily become animated at the
table, Vahedi was the No Limit Hold'em Player of the Year in 2001 and
2003. Ironically, though, Vahedi—whose passion is cars and trucks—believes the joy of
poker itself is long gone: It's the challenge of winning tournaments that drives him.

Vahedi says the best hand he ever played came during the $1,500 No Limit Hold'em
event at the 2001 World Series of Poker: "I lost almost 95 percent of my stack in one
hand. I was left with around $12,000 in chips. The average stack at the table was about
$180,000. Next hand is my big blind. The blinds were $1,500-$3,000, and I was dealt
A-6 offsuit.

"Nine out of ten players in my situation would've taken a stand with that kind of money.
It was raised and I gave it up. I just wasn't feeling good about it. I just wanted to have a
shot, even if an overcard hit. I had five or six hands to pick up the best of it."

On the button the next hand, Vahedi was dealt pocket 2's. He had about $8,000
remaining. "Then I took a stand. That way, I knew that even if someone had an ace or king
or anything like that, I still had outs. If a deuce hits, I can beat all the aces and the kings.

"There was a raise, a call, and I put all my money in there, which was less than the original raise. They started betting on the flop, and I knew one of them had an ace. But this time I knew that if my card came, I had a little hope.

"One of them had A-K, the other had A-Q. An ace and a queen both hit on the flop, but a deuce came on the turn. That's exactly what I wanted to happen. I made the right decision giving up almost one-third of my stack before I caught deuces."

After tripling up on that hand, Vahedi picked up several small pots, kept pushing all in, then, with a decent-size stack, waited for a hand and doubled up on someone who bluffed at him. By the end, he had captured his first World Series of Poker bracelet.

THE RAKE

In general, A-6 is not really a raising hand, so it is certainly not an all-in hand unless you are absolutely down to the felt. But because so many players overrate and overplay aces, almost everybody would have shoved their last chips into the pot with Vahedi's hand.

But he refused, and here's why: If someone else had been playing an ace, it likely would have been bigger than Vahedi's kicker 6, which meant he would pretty much be drawing dead. But in having some luck in getting dealt a small pocket pair at that time, Vahedi rightly figured the cards he needed to double or triple up wouldn't be counterfeited by one of his opponents.

The chances of flopping a set when you have a pocket pair are about 12 percent, which is bad enough to scare off a lot of players from trying to play small pairs in No Limit Hold'em unless they have position. There are two big reasons for this: If you miss the flop, then every overcard might beat you, and even if you flop a set, you run the risk of set over set if someone holds a pocket pair of an overcard on the board.

But small pairs can be a particularly wonderful weapon in Limit poker. If you're playing at a table where every ace calls but very few players raise, you have a chance to limp in and buy a cheap opportunity to flop a set. If the flop misses you, it is an easy hand to get away from. But if you hit your set, you can play aggressively against people who lack the discipline to lay down big cards, because Limit is a big-card game.

Re-buys: A tournament in which you can go broke and pay for another buy-in to continue playing. The number of rebuys for each player can be preset or can be limited to a particular number of blind levels. After the rebuy period, there is usually one add-on option, where players are allowed to buy more chips equal to the buy-in. Such tournaments generate a lot of action because players know they are not eliminated if they lose all their chips. **Counterfeited:** In Hold'em, it refers to having the same card as an opponent. In Omaha, it refers to holding a low card that also hits the board.

♠♦ DAVID WILLIAMS ♥♣

DAVID WILLIAMS CAME SO CLOSE. HE WAS HEADS-UP AND SO CLOSE to ascending to poker's greatest title in the 2004 World Series of Poker championship event, battling past every one of the nearly 2,600 entrants before **Greg Raymer** busted him to cop the bracelet and the $5 million first prize. Still, for the then twenty-three-year-old Williams, $3.5 million was a lovely parting gift.

The second-place finish was even more impressive for a kid who estimates he hadn't been in more than ten brick-and-mortar card rooms before coming to his first World Series. Let alone for a kid who danced through the largest field in poker history by drawing on his experience in playing Magic: The Gathering, a strategy game that combines elements of chess, bridge, and poker, and features a competitive tour that landed Williams in more than thirty countries.

There must be something to Magic, and there must be something to Williams, as well. He spent a semester at Princeton, where he got good grades, before returning to Dallas a little homesick and ready to enroll at nearby Southern Methodist University.

Williams became known for his black-shaded, black-rimmed sunglasses and stock-still look at the table, as well for as his tight relationship with mother, Shirley, away from it. Shirley remains her son's biggest fan, but Williams has since ditched the sunglasses. "I found it's more valuable to get the face time on TV and be recognized," he says, then adds with a laugh, "I'm so pretty, I have to make sure people see me."

Even with his eyes shaded, the poker world certainly saw Williams at the 2004 World Series of Poker main event, where he found the best hand he ever played.

"Two days before the final table, I started with a decent amount of chips and I was losing a lot of chips, hands were going bad, and I was depressed. My stack went from huge to small. I needed something to happen. It folds to the guy on the button, who I just dumped a lot of my chips to, and he makes a raise, which I kind of figure is a steal. I'm in the small blind and I look down and see two black aces, and I'm thinking, 'Oh, finally, this is it.'

"I re-raised him, doubling his raise. He called, and I think, 'Thank God I got some action. Now let's hope they hold up.'"

The flop came A-10-7, ace of hearts, and 10 and 7 of spades. "I bet out a small amount, kind of act out, look at him, look at my chips, and pick up my hand tentatively—put up a weak bet. The guy thinks and raises me. I kind of think and keep looking back at my hand, and I just call him.

"The turn comes the 8 of spades. Part of me is worried he may have made a flush, but

I'm also thinking, What would he have raised with that would've allowed him to make a flush here? Because he couldn't have ace-something for a flush draw because I have the ace of spades. So I figure he has a bigger pair. Hopefully he has a set, so I'm still happy because I have top set and a flush draw.

Brick-and-mortar: A physical card room, as opposed to an online card room out there in cyberspace.

"I check and he bets the same amount he raised me—a big amount, I don't remember exactly how much. We had really deep stacks. I re-raised three times his big raise, and he goes all in real fast. I call.

"Whenever that happens, they hold the hands. They don't turn them over. They call the camera crew and have it come over and they get ready. So they say, 'Okay, we have an all in here.' They call the camera crew over, set up, and they say, 'Turn the hands over.' They say, 'David Williams has a set of aces with a flush draw,' and then they say the other guy 'has a 7-8 and is drawing dead,' and they shut the cameras down and walk off.

"It doubled me up. I was down to $400,000-$500,000. It put me back up near a million. It was wonderful."

THE RAKE

The line on aces is that you can win a small pot with them, but you can also lose a big pot with them. So, the main thing to remember with aces is getting full value. And you can't get much better value than the way Williams got his opponent to match his stack.

He could have just called and hidden the strength of his hand before seeing the flop. But he was happy to win the pot right there when he really needed to win because, well, we've all heard stories about getting aces cracked. So Williams re-raised to see if his opponent was indeed on a steal, and his opponent called, perhaps thinking Williams was on tilt after dumping a good amount of chips to the same opponent.

After the flop, Williams went into a Hollywood act—looking tentative, checking his hand—to feign weakness, because now he had decided to make his opponent think that he was indeed on a steal. The reality is, Williams determined he needed to milk this hand to the river to get the most out of his aces, an example of thinking several plays ahead instead of just getting to the next card.

When the 8 of spades turned, Williams had concern that he was against a flush, but here is where the analytical mind of a top player shows itself. Williams recapped the betting, and it went like this: In order to bet the flush, Williams' opponent would have had to have something good to raise with and then call Williams' re-raise pre-flop, then re-raise post-flop, but he could not have the nut-flush card because Williams held it, so he was probably up against big cards or a medium set, and he had those beat.

In the end, Williams was content to check and let his opponent essentially bet Williams' hand, showing weakness as part of setting a trap. Williams' opponent played right into it, shoving all his chips into the middle when he was already beaten.

♠♦ ROBERT WILLIAMSON III ♥♣

WHEN ROBERT WILLIAMSON III SAYS HE HUSTLED AT AN EARLY AGE, HE MEANS EARLY—
as in five years old, when his father took him to card and dice games.

"I was already hustling sandwiches and drinks to the players for tips," Williamson recalls. "My mom didn't necessarily approve of this. It involved about one night a week staying up all night. She didn't like the idea of a young kid staying up all night, but what my dad was teaching me was work ethic and the art of the hustle." Learning card games took a little longer, however.

"When I was really young, until I understood gambling really well, my father and my little sister used to beat us up mercilessly in family poker games," Williamson says, remembering his early Texas years. "It killed me to lose because the losers had to go to bed and the winners got to keep the money. Once you were out, you were out. There were so many nights where I didn't get to see who won because I was out of money and had to go to bed. I learned at a very young age the idea of the game was to win."

If that kind of education seems unconventional, then consider this pedagogical method: "I started playing for adult stakes—$10-$20, $20-$40—when I was thirteen at a truck stop in Vegas," Williamson says. "My dad would take me out of school twice a year to go to Vegas for two or three weeks. He had a deal worked out with my school that he would take me on educational trips. So I studied everything from the Grand Canyon to Hoover Dam, Reno, Silver City—we did everything historic you could do in the state of Nevada. Everything from the border of the state of Texas to Nevada, I did as a child."

On those rare occasions when the colorful Williamson actually showed up at his high school in Texas, he was scalping high-end tickets for concerts. Art of the hustle, indeed. In college at Angelo State University, Williamson started a real estate company. But he was spending more time playing poker, so he sold the company and hit a card room in Tunica, Mississippi, finding a game he could crush to the point that he ended up owning a piece of ten Pancake Kettle House restaurants as an investment.

But that was too much like work. So Williamson ditched the restaurants and set about traveling the world on the big-time poker circuit in 1999. By 2002, he had won his first World Series of Poker bracelet, capturing the Pot Limit Omaha championship. The next year, he finished third in the same event, while winning the Mid-American Classic No Limit Hold'em title and the World Poker Open Pot Limit Omaha championship. In 2004, Williamson just missed his second Pot Limit Omaha bracelet, finishing second to Chau Giang.

Williamson says the best hand he ever played came on the final deal of the Pot Limit Omaha event at the World Series of Poker in 2002, when he won his first bracelet.

"I got heads-up with Patrick Bruel, who is the number one singer/actor in France. But he's also a great poker player. Chau Giang and **Johnny Chan** were also at the final table with us, so it was an all-star cast. There were twenty-two bracelets represented at the final table, and I didn't have one yet. One other guy and I were the only ones who didn't have a bracelet.

"We got heads-up and we had about the same amount of chips. We go back and forth for maybe three hands. The fourth hand, let me set the scene: I'm on the button, the blinds are somewhere around $2,000-$4,000, we both have about $200,000-something in chips in front of us, so we both have probably half a million between us. I have slightly more chips than him.

"I limped on the button with 3-5-7-J double-suited, spades and clubs, which only come into the story because there were neither on the board. I limped to make it $4,000 and he raised it $8,000 more, so I called $12,000 pre-flop." With $24,000 in the pot, the flop came 4-6-10, two diamonds, and a heart.

"It's a good flop for a wraparound with the 3-5-7. I decided to play this hand very cautiously because I put him on a big pair—aces or kings—and he could have the nut-flush draw or the king-high flush draw, and if he does, he's still a favorite over my wraparound.

"He bet the pot on the flop. I beat him into the pot. I'm trying to hold him off on the turn in case it comes a blank by betting so fast. Now there's $72,000 in the pot.

"The turn card came an 8 of hearts, so it put both flushes out there that I didn't have, and it put out a higher straight. He led instantly, betting the pot, $72,000. I made an instant judgment that he didn't have the nut straight. I figured he had a big pair and one of the two flush draws. Now, with one card to come, I'm roughly 2.5-1 favorite. I said, 'Raise,' and before I could say anything else, he pushed all of his chips in. I don't know if I was going to raise enough to cover him, but as soon as he pushed the rest of his chips in, I pushed the rest of my chips in. Before I could do anything, he says, 'Do you have a straight?' I said, 'Yes.' He says, 'Good hand,' and he mucked his hand. It's a half-million-dollar pot and he tried to muck his hand.

"Well, every final hand in the World Series is recorded for history, so they grabbed the hand from him. They wouldn't let him muck the hand. So, I go, 'Oh, my god, they're making him show the hand. Maybe he misread his hand. If he turns over a winning hand, I could lose. He already said he's dead.'

"There are two flush draws out there, there's a higher straight out there, and he says, 'Good hand.' I thought for sure I was going to have to fade at least 10 or 12 outs. I won the hand on the turn when I made the straight. I don't remember what the river card was. It didn't matter. He was drawing dead. He had K-K-A and I'm going to say the last

Double-suited: When your four-card Omaha hand has two cards of one suit and two of another. **Wraparound:** In Omaha, an open-ended straight, needing one card on the top or bottom to make the hand. **Fade:** To dodge cards that would give an opponent a better hand.

card was a 9, but it was a rainbow hand, and he was drawing dead. That's how I won my first bracelet."

THE RAKE

The fact that Bruel played only four hands heads-up against Williamson tells you that Bruel didn't think he could outplay his opponent and was probably worried that he would get picked apart the longer it went. Bruel gambled that he could choose one spot with some big cards and crush Williamson.

The advantage to this style is you put tremendous pressure on your opponent. The disadvantage is you don't have time to feel out your opponent to know when the best spot for such an aggressive move is.

Pre-flop, Bruel was a 55-45 favorite to win the hand with his pair of kings, so he made a solid pot-size bet that could have won the hand right there. He was getting in as much money as he could when he believed he had the best of it.

Williamson called Bruel's bet because he was double-suited and held straight possibilities. On the 4-6-10 flop, even though it was all red and Williamson held all black, Williamson became a 62-38 percent favorite. Bruel's pot-sized bet of $24,000 was another attempt to win the pot immediately, or at least represent a flush draw.

Williamson's quick call was a move you see many times at a table when a player on only a draw tries to represent a strong hand of his own to counter an opponent's aggressive play. It is a reverse tell. In the face of such pressure, Williamson was willing to take one more card to see if he could make his hand. In a big card came, Williamson likely would have mucked his hand to any bet and gone on to the next deal because he would have been too big of an underdog with just one card to come.

But when an 8 fell on the turn, Williamson made his wraparound. Then, when Bruel pushed all in before Williamson even announced his raise amount, Williamson realized he probably had the best hand and figured he would have to dodge about 12 of the possible cards that might make Bruel's hand.

It turned out, the hand was over. Bruel was drawing dead and had committed the grave poker error of making his biggest bets when he didn't have the odds on his side.

♠♦ THE RIVER ♥♣

HOWARD LEDERER LIKES TO SAY THAT POKER IS A GAME OF INCOMPLETE INFORMATION, and certainly the Professor of Poker is correct. The key to making that information as complete as possible is knowing that everything matters—cards, chip counts, position, tells, betting patterns, pot odds, and especially reading people.

In *The Best Hand I Ever Played*, you have seen fifty-two examples of how some of the best players in the world prioritize those components throughout a hand. How you sort through those different elements and how you weigh their importance in a particular situation will determine success or failure. So adapt your game to those parts that make sense to you. As you become more comfortable in making your game more creative, adapt a few more.

There is, of course, one other element that runs through these stories, one factor that is an undeniable aspect of a world-class poker player: heart. Heart most obviously surfaces in the hands in which players came to believe they can compete at the highest levels, such as Doyle Brunson calling down poker master Johnny Moss with just a jack-high, or a fairly green Chip Reese jumping into one of the biggest cash games in the world with more optimism than bankroll. Whether you are playing on television or in a buddy's basement, you can learn the value of developing the confidence to trust your instincts and believe in your game.

Naturally, heart plays a big role in the many bluffs described in these pages, such as Dewey Tomko's quick thinking in a hand against a gun-waving, life-threatening opponent, Antonio "The Magician" Esfandiari's walk on the wild side as he put to the test an opponent holding a better hand, and Daniel Negreanu's classic lesson in putting another player on a hand and finding the perfect amount to bet him into folding. These top players all agree that the key to pulling off a successful bluff is the ability to play your lesser holdings the way you already have played the big hand you are attempting to represent.

Heart also plays a considerable role in the decision to fold, especially when holding a big hand, such as Phil Gordon laying down pocket kings during the final two tables of the 2001 World Series of Poker main event when he correctly deduced that he was facing pocket aces, or Annie Duke mucking pocket 10's to stay alive and go on to win the $2 million winner-take-all World Series of Poker Tournament of Champions event in 2004. That many top players cite laydowns as the best hands they ever played points up the importance of developing the ability to know when you're beaten and the willingness to make the correct, if painful, move.

So consider yourself armed for battle at the tables, whether it is in your home game, during a trip to Vegas, or perhaps even after you've taken that ultimate leap and entered a tournament, where you are likely to meet any or all of the people in this book.

♠♦ POKER HAND RANKINGS ♥♣

Royal flush: A-K-Q-J-10 of the same suit.

Straight flush: Five consecutive cards of the same suit.

Four of a kind: Four cards of the same rank.

Full house: Three of a kind and two of a kind.

Flush: Five cards of the same suit, but not in order.

Straight: Five consecutive cards, but not all of the same suit.

Three of a kind: Three cards of the same rank.

Two pair: Two pairs of different ranks.

Pair: Two cards of the same rank.

High card: An unpaired hand in which the value is determined by the highest-ranking card. The ace is the highest card, followed by the king, etc.

♠♦ GLOSSARY ♥♣

Ace-to-Five Triple Draw Lowball: A five-card game in which you try to make the best low hand—in this case A-2-3-4-5—and can draw up to three times, with betting on each round.

Aces up: A hand with two pair, one of which is aces.

All in: To move all of your chips into the pot.

Ante: A forced bet players make before a hand is dealt to prompt action.

Bad beat: To lose a hand when you are the favorite. It's particularly bad when it happens on the river.

Bet into: To bet ahead of the player who has represented the strongest hand.

Betting out: To lead the betting.

Big bet: In a Limit game, it is the size of the bet on the last two rounds; in a No Limit game, it is the size of the big blind.

Big blind: See blinds.

Big Slick: A-K in the hole.

Black chip game: A table where the lowest denomination of chips is $100, which is the black chip in most casinos.

Blank: A card that does not affect the strength of a hand.

Blank ace: In Omaha, where you must use exactly two cards from your hand and exactly three cards from the board, a blank ace refers to holding the ace but no other card of the same suit, thus preventing you from making a flush.

Blinds: Two forced bets prior to any cards being dealt to encourage action in each hand. The small blind is posted by the player to the left of the dealer button. The big blind is posted by the player two seats to the left of the dealer. The amount of the small blind is half of the big blind. Other players wishing to participate in the hand must at least match the amount of the big blind. In tournaments, blinds are raised at predetermined intervals, usually every ninety minutes or two hours.

Board: The common cards turned face up.

Box: Many poker rooms have something akin to safe-deposit boxes where players can store chips so they don't have to go through the cash exchange buy-in routine. Also refers to a chip rack in front of a dealer.

Brick-and-mortar: A physical card room, as opposed to an online card room.

Bring it in: A forced first bet. In high-low split games, it is the lowest card that makes the first bet; in high-only games, it is the highest card that leads the betting.

Button: A hockey puck-like disk that says "Dealer." It designates the last player to receive cards and the last player to act after the flop. It is the best position at the table, which is why it rotates clockwise on each deal, ensuring that each player gets the advantage the button provides.

Call: To match a bet.

Capped: The maximum number of raises on each round.

Case money: The last of anything. In a deck, if there are three aces out and you draw the fourth, you've drawn the case ace. The last of your money is case money.

Cashed: To have finished in a payout spot in a tournament.

Cash game: The most conventional form of poker, whether it is in a casino or your basement. You buy chips and play. If you go broke, you can buy more chips. In a tournament, when you go broke, you leave the table. Cash games also are referred to as side games.

Check: To pass on opening the betting in a particular round.

Check-raise: An aggressive move where a player first checks, then waits for an opponent to bet, and when it becomes his turn to act again, he proceeds to raise.

Cold call: When a player matches an opponent's raise.

Come over the top: To re-raise a huge amount, usually all in.

Coordinated board: The common cards work strongly in various combinations to make a hand, say a straight, a flush, or a full house, or some combination of the three.

Counterfeited: In Hold'em, it refers to having the same card as an opponent. In Omaha, it refers to holding a low card that also hits the board.

Crying call: Matching your opponent's last bet, even though you believe you are beaten.

Cutoff: The table position one to the right of the dealer button.

Dead money: Derogatory term referring to amateurs entering poker tournaments. So-called "dead money" players won the World Series of Poker main events in 2002 (Robert Varkonyi), 2003 (Chris Moneymaker), and 2004 (Greg Raymer).

Define a hand: Making a bet to force a response from an opponent that gives a player a sense of his relative strength.

Deuce: Another name for a 2.

Deuce-to-Seven Draw: A type of lowball where the best hand—in this case, 7-5-4-3-2—would be the worst in most other games. Games with a draw allow you to throw away cards from your hand and be dealt the same number of new cards from the deck.

Double-suited: When your four-card Omaha hand has two cards of one suit and two of another.

Drawing dead: To have lost the hand even with a card or two to come.

Drawing hand: Holding cards that could potentially make a straight or a flush, but haven't yet.

Draw out: To have the remaining board cards make your hand.

Drown on the river: To lose on the last common card turned face up. Where bad beat stories are made.

Early position: Generally considered one of the first three betting spots in any hand.

Fade: To dodge cards that would give an opponent a better hand.

Fake flush: Holding four cards to a flush when there are no common cards left to come.

Fifth Street: See River.

Final table: Poker's equivalent of the playoffs. This is where the big payoffs are because this is where the tournament is won. In the World Series of Poker, the final table consists of nine players. In World Poker Tour events, the final table consists of six players.

First seat: Also known as first position, it is the first player to act in a given round of betting.

Fish: Bad players; also known as dead money.

Five Card Stud: A game in which each player gets one card down and four cards up with betting after each exposed card.

Flop: The first three common cards in Hold'em or Omaha, which are revealed at once.

Flopped a hand: To develop a good holding after the first three common cards are exposed.

Flush draw: Four cards to completing a flush.

Fourth Street: See Turn.

Freerolling: When you already have the nut low or nut high in a split game, you are getting a free shot to improve your hand enough to also win the other half of the pot.

Full: To make a full house, i.e., 2's full of queens.

Gutshot: An inside straight draw in which one card will make the hand. For instance, if you have a 2-3-5-6, you need a 4 to complete a straight. Also known as a belly buster.

Heads-up: Playing one-on-one; usually referring to the last two players in a tournament.

High-Low Split: The highest hand splits the pot with the lowest hand.

H.O.E.: An acronym for a tournament of rotating games—Hold'em, Omaha-8-or-better, and Seven Card Stud Hi-Low Split games—that change at prescribed times, usually each half-hour. (The "E" stands for eight or better.)

H.O.R.S.E: An acronym for a tournament of rotating games—Hold'em, Omaha 8-or-Better, Razz, Seven Card Stud Hi-Low Split. (The "E" stands for eight or better.)

House: Another name for the casino; the host of the game.

Ignorant end of the straight: Holding the card or cards on the small end of the straight.

Implied pot odds: Not just the amount of money in the pot, but the additional amount you can reasonably expect to be bet into the pot by the end based on the way players have represented their hands so far. Pot odds are the percentage of your chances of hitting an unseen card that can make your hand versus the cost of your bet compared to amount of money in the pot. Implied pots odds are the percentage of your chances of hitting an unseen card compared to the cost of your bet versus the amount of money that will be in the pot by the end.

Kicker: An unmatched card used to break ties.

Late position: Generally considered the spot at the table where the button sits, and the two positions to the right of it.

Lay down: To fold a hand.

Lead out: To open the betting; to lead out into the original bettor or the raiser is a way of pressuring the opponent and representing strength.

Limit Omaha: Limit poker is a game that has preset betting amounts. For example, a $10-$20 game means bets or raises are limited to $10 on the first two rounds, then increase to $20 on the next two rounds. Omaha is a game in which you are dealt four hole cards with five cards to be turned face up as in Hold'em—three cards on the flop and one each on the turn and the river—but you must use exactly two cards from your hand and exactly three cards from the board to make your five-card poker hand.

Limp: To call the minimum bet.

Loose-aggressive: A term to describe a player who will go after a lot of pots with some-times marginal holdings.

Loose game: Many players seeing the flop and playing marginal cards.

Made hand: A hand that doesn't need improvement to win.

Maniac: A super-aggressive player who seems to be raising every pot from any position with any two cards. A maniac will run over a table unless you play back at him.

Medium-limit: Generally refers to games with $20-$40 and $30-$60 betting limits.

Middle full house: When your set in a full house is comprised of 6's, 7's, 8's, or 9's.

Middle position: Generally referring to seats 4, 5, and 6 in the betting order of a particular round.

Muck: To fold a hand; "the muck" refers to the pile of cards that are folded or unused.

No Limit Hold'em: In Hold'em, players are dealt two hole cards, followed by a maximum of five board cards (the first three exposed cards are the flop, the next card is the turn, the final card is the river). There are four rounds of betting: After each player receives hole cards, the flop, the turn and the river. In No Limit, the minimum bet is the size of the big blind. The maximum is all your chips, and you can bet all of them at any time.

Nut flush: The best possible flush based on what the board is showing.

Nuts: The best possible hand.

Offsuit: Cards of different suits.

Omaha-8-or-Better: Played like straight Omaha—four hole cards, five board cards, you must use exactly two cards from your hand and exactly three cards from the board to make your five-card poker hand—but the pot is split between the best high hand and the best low hand. The low hand, however, must start with a card no higher than an 8 (i.e., 8-5-6-2-A.) Straights and flushes are irrelevant when determining the low hand. You can use the same cards to make your low hand and your high hand or different cards for each half of the pot. For instance, A-2-3-4-5 can be used as the best low hand and a straight for the high hand. If there is no low hand, the high hand wins the pot.

One-gappers: Cards separated by one rank, i.e., 9-7 and 8-6.

On tilt: To play out of control, usually the result of a bad beat or a bad decision that cost a player a lot of chips.

Open-ended straight draw: To have four consecutive cards and need a card at either end to complete the straight, i.e., having 5-6-7-8 and needing either a 9 or a 4 to make the hand.

Out of position: When your spot in the betting rotation comes before your opponents, meaning you don't have the advantage of seeing all the action before you must make a move.

Outs: The unexposed cards that would make your hand. If you have no outs when there are still cards to be exposed on the board, you are said to be drawing dead.

Overbet: To make a bet more than the total amount in the pot.

Overcard: A card in your hand that is higher than any card on the board, or a card on the board that is higher than the best card in your hand.

Overpair: Matching hole cards that are higher than the best card on the board.

Pai Gow Poker: A casino table game in which each player is dealt seven cards and tries to make a five-card hand and a two-card hand that beat the dealer using traditional hand rankings. If both hands beat the dealer, the player wins. If both lose, the house wins. If only one hand wins, it is a push. Dealers win ties. The deck includes a joker that can be used as an ace or to complete straights and flushes.

Phony flush: In Omaha, holding an ace but no other card of that suit in your hand, meaning you cannot win with a flush because you must use two cards from your down cards and three from the board.

Pit boss: The person in charge of the dealers at table games in casinos.

Play back: To re-raise an opponent. Sometimes it is done to reinforce strength, sometimes it is done to make an opponent doubt the strength of his hand.

Playing fast: Aggressively betting and raising pots.

Pocket pair: Matching cards in the hole.

Pocket rockets: Another name for a pair of aces in the hole.

Position: Your spot in the betting rotation as determined by the dealer button, which moves clockwise on each hand. The later your position, the better.

Positional raise: A play usually made from late position when no one has entered or raised the pot.

Pot Limit: A game where the biggest bet cannot exceed the amount of money in the pot. Pot Limit games frequently reach No Limit-like proportions by the river.

Pre-flop: The first round of betting before the first three common cards are exposed.

Price: Pot odds.

Protector: An object that players put on their cards when they play a hand. It can be anything from a stack of chips to a good-luck charm to even fossils, which is what Greg Raymer used in the 2004 World Series of Poker main event to become known as Fossilman. The function of protectors is to make sure the dealer doesn't grab your cards and shove them into the muck, thereby killing your hand.

Putting an opponent on a hand: The ability to determine which cards another player is holding based on his betting pattern, his position at the table from which he is making those bets, and his history of betting in other situations. You are trying to figure out how strong or weak a hand you're up against.

Quads over quads: A four-of-a-kind beating another four-of-a-kind.

Rags: Low or bad cards that don't make a good hand.

Rainbow: A flop of three different suits.

Raised the pot: The maximum raise in a Pot Limit game.

Raising blind: To raise without looking at your cards. Also known as raising in the dark.

Razz: A variation on Seven Card Stud in which the low hand wins.

Rebuys: A tournament in which you can go broke and pay for another buy-in to continue playing. The number of rebuys for each player can be preset or it can be limited to a particular number of blind levels. After the rebuy period, there is one add-on option, where players are allowed to buy more chips equal to the buy-in. Such tournaments generate a lot of action because players know they are not eliminated if they lose all their chips.

Represent: To bet as if you have made a good hand based on the common cards.

Reverse tell: Faking a physical or verbal mannerism to deceive an opponent into thinking you're strong when you're weak, or vice versa.

River: The last card dealt in a poker hand. In Hold'em and Omaha, it is also known as fifth street.

Rolled up: When your first three cards match in Seven Card Stud, i.e., when your two hole cards are 6's and your first exposed card is also a 6.

Runner-runner: The last two common cards—fourth street and fifth street—usually used when both cards are needed to make a hand and both cards in fact do come.

Running cards: See runner-runner.

Satellite: A way to win entry into a tournament. Satellites have reduced entry fees, but the catch is you have to win a single-table or multi-table tournament to gain a spot in the bigger event.

Second pair: Pairing the middle card in the flop with a hole card; also known as middle pair.

Semi-bluff: Betting out or raising when you have some kind of hand, but not as big as you are making it appear. It's not a total bluff because you still have some outs that would allow you to win the pot.

Set: Three of a kind.

Seven Card Stud: Each player receives his first two cards down, the next four cards up, and the last card down. There is a round of betting after each up card and the last down card. Players use the seven cards to make the best five-card hand.

Seven Card Stud Limit High-Low Split: A Seven Card Stud game with preset betting limits where the best high hand splits the pot with the best low hand.

Short-handed: Playing at a table that is not full.

Side-action games: Another name for cash games that take place while a tournament is going on.

Slow-playing: To pass on opening the betting despite holding a powerful hand. It's usually done with aces or kings, or after flopping a set or a nut flush. The idea is to induce a player with lesser holdings to read you as weak as a way of trapping the player into betting.

Small blind: See blinds.

Smooth-call: To match an opponent's bet. It is usually made by a player who would ordinarily consider raising.

Stack: The amount of chips a player has.

Steal: To represent a hand you don't actually have. It's another way of saying you're trying to win the pot with a bluff.

Stone nuts: The absolute best possible hand.

Suck out: To have the worst hand heading into the river, but drawing a card that makes your hand a winner.

Suited: Hole cards of the same suit.

Suited connectors: Consecutive cards of the same suit.

Table image: How you are perceived in a game based on your personality and your betting habits. For instance, a loose-aggressive table image comes from playing or raising almost as many hands as a maniac, while a weak-tight player has a table image of playing only premium hands and not playing them as aggressively.

Tell: A physical or verbal mannerism that gives away the strength or weakness of your hand.

Three-bet: A term used in Limit games; a player makes a bet, another player raises, thus making it two bets to play, then a third player re-raises, making it three bets to continue.

Tight-aggressive: A player who plays few hands, but bets them aggressively when he does.

Tight game: Few players seeing the flop and betting only premium hands.

Top set: The best possible three-of-a-kind.

Trap: To feign weakness with a strong hand in hopes of getting your opponent to bet big.

Trey: Another name for a 3.

Triple up: To go all in and get called by two players, and then win the hand. You end up with three times the chips you started the hand with.

Turn: The fourth of five common cards turned face up in Hold'em and Omaha. Also known as fourth street.

Underbet: A bet that is less than expected for the size of the pot. Sometimes it is a strategy ploy to get an opponent to call. Sometimes it is a probe bet to determine the strength of your opponent's hand.

Under the gun: The first player to act in a hand.

Unsuited: Cards of different suits.

Wheel: A straight consisting of A-2-3-4-5; also known as a baby straight.

Wired pair: Same as a pocket pair.

World Poker Tour: An international circuit of poker events that is broadcast on the Travel Channel. It was created in 2002 and revolutionized televised poker through the use of tiny cameras that reveal each player's hole cards.

World Series of Poker: The most famous poker tournament in the world. It began in 1970 when Benny Binion drew his Texas poker pals together at his Las Vegas casino, Binion's Horseshoe, for several days of poker events. The champion was determined by a vote of the players. Poker legend Johnny Moss was the first champion. After that, the champion became the player holding all the chips in the final event, which cost $10,000 to enter. The buy-in for the main event remains $10,000, but there are more than 30 events at different buy-in levels for which the winner gets a gold bracelet. Abbreviated WSOP.

Wraparound: In Omaha, an open-ended straight, needing one card on the top or bottom to make the hand.

♠♦ ACKNOWLEDGMENTS ♥♣

It starts with Bill Adee, my sports editor at the *Chicago Tribune*. With the approval of *Tribune* Editor Ann Marie Lipinski and Associate Managing Editor/Sports Dan McGrath, Bill came to me in the spring of 2004 and proposed the idea for a weekly poker column with hopes that it would become syndicated. The column happened.

The syndication happened. And this book happened as a result of having access to the best poker players in the world.

Speaking of the best poker players in the world, I must thank all of them for their time and insight. The closer you get to their world, the farther you feel from their level of play. Special thanks to "Miami" John Cernuto. He was the first top professional player I approached with the question: "What's the best hand you ever played?"—and he laughed and then said, "That's a good idea," and then gave me a hand where he bluffed out four other players.

After that, I must thank Greg Dinkin and Frank Scatoni, the brains of Venture Literary. Talk about poker expertise. With their help and guidance, this book became far better than I imagined.

As for Michael Solomon, my editor, and Chris Raymond, the editor-in-chief at ESPN Books, they didn't see just a book, they saw a multimedia experience. Michael's player-centric focus and story-telling sensibilities gave these chapters the kind of personality that I knew existed but wasn't sure I could produce. With his prodding, I did. Michael's and Chris' support, help, and vision is the best set of trips that any poker author could draw to.

Nobody who writes this kind of detailed book gets it all right to start with. Facts need to be checked. Numbers must match. For helping me get it as right as humanly possible, I wish to thank Jordan Brenner, Jason Catania, and Michael Mott at ESPN research for their tireless work, relentless questioning, and enthusiastic effort.

Because many of the hands in this book came from televised events, I want to applaud ESPN's *World Series of Poker*, the Travel Channel's World Poker Tour, and FoxSportsNet's *Championship Poker at the Plaza* for their terrific presentations. And because many of these hands required significant research, I want to note the clarity and depth offered in *Poker: The Real Deal*, by Phil Gordon and Jonathan Grotenstein; *Poker Aces*, by Ron Rose; *Play Poker Like the Pros*, by Phil Hellmuth; and *The Championship Table* by Dana Smith, Tom McEvoy and Ralph Wheeler.

A special mention for Vel and Jerry, who might not be my parents, but still provided love and support—not to mention room and board—as I tracked down poker players on the west coast.

Finally, and most important, I want to thank Karen, Allison, and Brandon, who dealt with my crazy hours, long road trips, and a lot of time in the garage amid cigar smoke to make this happen.

Steve Rosenbloom
June 2005

♠ ♦ ABOUT THE AUTHOR ♥ ♣

Steve Rosenbloom is the syndicated poker columnist for the *Chicago Tribune*. His column is featured in papers from coast to coast, and he also writes regular column online for the ESPN Poker Club. A longtime sportswriter and editor, Rosenbloom covers the World Poker Tour and the World Series of Poker, and has been playing the game since he was old enough to see over the table.

PHOTO CREDITS

FRONT COVER:

WILLIAMS: Steve Grayson/ WireImage.com GORDON: John Sciulli/WireImage.com DUKE: Gail Oskin/WireImage.com LAAK: Steve Grayson/WireImage.com. RAYMER: Steve Grayson/WireImage.com. BRUNSON: Bob Gevinski/WireImage.com.

BACK COVER:

Author Photo: Glenn Kaupert/Chicago Tribune.

PLAYERS:

ARIEH: Steve Grayson/WireImage.com. AWADA: Courtesy of Eric Harkins/Image Masters PDI. BERMAN: Courtesy of Eric Harkins/Image Masters PDI. BRUNSON: Bob Gevinski/WireImage.com. CHAN: Chuck Toussieng/WireImage.com. CHERNUTO: Jodi Shapiro. CLOUTIER: Courtesy of Pamela Shandell/Image Masters PDI. CORKINS: Jim Rogash/WireImage.com. DE KNIJFF: Courtesy of Eric Harkins/Image Masters PDI. DEEB: Courtesy of Eric Harkins/Image Masters PDI. DUKE: Gail Oskin/WireImage.com. ESFANDI-ARI: Christina Elliott/WireImage.com. FISCHMAN: Courtesy of Eric Harkins/Image Masters PDI. FLACK: Courtesy of Eric Harkins/Image Masters PDI. GOEHRING: Steve Grayson/WireImage.com. GORDON: John Sciulli/WireImage.com. GRIFFIN: Courtesy of Eric Harkins/Image Masters PDI. HABIB: Courtesy of Eric Harkins/Image Masters PDI. HANSEN: Robert B. Stanton/WireImage.com. HARMAN: Jim Rogash/WireImage.com. HARRINGTON: Steve Grayson/WireImage.com. HOFF: Larry Grossman. JETT: Jodi Shapiro. JUDAH: Courtesy of Eric Harkins/Image Masters PDI. KELLER: Courtesy of Eric Harkins/Image Masters PDI. LAAK: Steve Grayson/ WireImage.com. LEDERER: Steve Grayson/WireImage.com. LIEBERT: Lester Cohen/WireImage.com. LINDGREN: Gail Oskin/WireImage.com. LUSKE: Larry Grossman. MATROS: Jodi Shapiro. McEVOY: Larry Grossman. MONEYMAKER: Phil Ellsworth. NEGREANU: Steve Grayson/WireImage.com. NG: Steve Grayson/WireImage.com. M. NGUYEN: Robert B. Stanton/WireImage.com. S. NGUYEN: Gail Oskin/WireImage.com. PHILLIPS: Larry Grossman. PRESTON: Jim Rogash/WireImage.com. RAYMER: Steve Grayson/WireImage.com. REESE: Steve Grayson/WireImage.com. ROSE: Jim Rogash/WireImage.com. SEIDEL: Steve Grayson/WireImage.com. SEXTON: Lester Cohen/WireImage.com. SHULMAN: Courtesy of Eric Harkins/Image Masters PDI. SHOTEN: Courtesy of Eric Harkins/Image Masters PDI. TOMKO: Jodi Shapiro. ULLIOTT: Courtesy of Eric Harkins/Image Masters PDI. VAHEDI: Courtesy of Eric Harkins / Image Masters PDI. WILLIAMS: Steve Grayson/ WireImage.com. THALER: Courtesy of Eric Harkins/Image Masters PDI. WILLIAMSON: Michael Schwartz/WireImage.com

ENDORSED BY
Annie Duke–Winner 2004 Tournament of Champions

WWW.ESPNSHOP.COM

Give your next poker night the look and feel of an official ESPN Poker Club event: Visit ESPNshop.com to purchase the complete line of ESPN Poker Club chip sets and accessories.

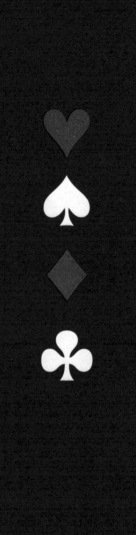